Learning the Landscape

Learning the Landscape

Inquiry-Based Activities for Comprehending and Composing

Fran Claggett
Louann Reid
Ruth Vinz

Boynton/Cook Publishers
Heinemann
Portsmouth, NH

Boynton/Cook Publishers
A subsidiary of Reed Elsevier Inc.
361 Hanover Street
Portsmouth, NH 03801-3912
Offices and agents throughout the world

Editor: Peter Stillman
Manufacturing: Louise Richardson
Cover photo: Renée M. Nicholls
Cover design: Joanne Tranchemontagne and Renée M. Nicholls

The authors and publisher wish to thank those who have generously given
permission to reprint material:

Pages 6, 7, 8, 10, 11, 13, 14: "Ask Me" and "Traveling Through the Dark" from
STORIES THAT COULD BE TRUE by William Stafford. Copyright © 1978 by
William Stafford. Reprinted by permission of the Estate of William Stafford.

Page 10: "To You Around Me" by William Stafford originally appeared in
NIGHTSUN, edited by Jorn K. Bramann. Copyright © William Stafford.
Reprinted by permission.
(Credit lines continued at the end of the book.)

Claggett, Mary Frances.
    Learning the landscape : inquiry-based activities for comprehending
    and composing / Fran Claggett, Louann Reid, Ruth Vinz.
        p.   cm.
    Includes bibliographical references and index.
    ISBN 0-86709-395-1 (alk. paper)
    1. Language arts (Secondary)—United States.   2. Reading (Sec-
ondary)—United States.   3. Reader-response criticism—United States.
4. High school students—United States—Diaries.   5. English language—
Composition and exercises—Study and teaching (Secondary)—United
States.   I. Reid, Louann.   II. Vinz, Ruth.   III. Title.
LB1631.C535   1996
428'.0071'2—dc20   96-20849
                                                                  CIP

Printed in the United States of America on acid-free paper
99 98 97 96   DA   1 2 3 4 5 6

Contents

Preface

Learning the Landscape: Inquiry-Based Activities for Comprehending and Composing provides projects that focus on your relationship to your surroundings, to your neighborhoods, and to the ecological system. Through the literature that you read and produce, you will explore how geographical and spiritual landscapes inform your sense of identity, community, and global understanding.

More or less obviously, a textbook reflects the values and beliefs of its authors. This text is no different. We value close reading of literature and careful attention to craft in the writing of literature. Yet, in many other ways, the book you're reading now does differ from the huge anthologies currently available.

Our overriding goal is to help you become transactive, discerning readers and thoughtful, perceptive writers. The way to approach this ideal, we decided, is by integrating the language arts as fully as possible. In this text, we consciously draw on many ways of learning that we have found useful to our students—observing, analyzing, imagining, and reflecting. Thus you'll find language and literature experiences structured so that you use writing, drawing, performing, and discussing to learn about what you're reading.

We believe that you as readers need to find something of yourself in every selection, defining yourself as you examine the text. We also believe that through the shared stories and poems that you read and write you will develop your understanding of how stories form and are transformed by human experience. This book offers texts from a variety of times and places written by professionals and students.

As you read and write, listen and speak, perform and draw, you will employ several language tools. Logs are a vital means for responding to the text. In logs and more sustained projects and papers, you are continually directed to extend your thinking beyond response and to engage in analysis, evaluation, and reflection. Performing and drawing are also powerful ways to read and interpret literature. Finally we give you guidelines for developing a portfolio that includes work completed in various media while using this textbook.

More and more teachers have expressed a need to accommodate various learning styles, provide opportunities for collaboration on problem-solving projects, and help you engage in a real negotiation with texts in both reading and writing. This book is designed to meet those needs.

Acknowledgments

We wish to thank our colleagues who have contributed to this text by engaging with us in the ongoing dialogue, the "grand conversation" about teaching and learning. Their names are too numerous to mention, but they extend from California to Florida, from New York to Colorado, from Idaho to Georgia, and points in between. We also wish to thank the many students whose patience and enthusiasm led us to refinements in our design of better ways to help them excel in and enjoy the processes of comprehending and composing. A special thanks goes to those students whose work appears in these pages.

Particular mention must go to Scott Lindsten and Juhl Wojahn, who carefully transcribed student work; to Jean Wendelin, who patiently tracked down difficult sources for permission to reprint works; and to Judith Hargrave, whose close reading and diligent copyediting ensured completion of the final manuscript. We are grateful to Madge Holland for reading and rereading the text, always with an eye toward clarity and classroom usefulness.

No acknowledgments would be complete without mentioning the work of those researchers and thinkers whose work has so powerfully affected our thinking about teaching and learning. Of most immediate relevance to this book is Louise M. Rosenblatt, for her seminal work with a transactional approach to reading and writing. Jimmy Britton's vision played a vital role in our understanding of language and learning. The thinking and writing of John Mayher, Dan Kirby, Robert Scholes, and Bob Probst are also implicated in the concepts and projects that we present in this text.

Finally we want to thank Bob Boynton and Peter Stillman for envisioning and trusting that there were books that *should* be written—books that depart from the standard fare available to both teachers and students. They have questioned, provoked, and supported us through all of the stages that led to the publication of *Learning the Landscape*.

1

Exploring the Possibilities: An Introduction

*I*n *Learning the Landscape,* you'll observe, record, read, and write about the landscapes that we live in and those we create for ourselves through our actions and our visions. We use the word *landscape* in a metaphoric way to include not only the physical features of the land but also the neighborhoods, communities, and societies that we've created. We'll ask you to examine how the landscapes in which we live shape us as well as how we shape the landscapes. Our powers of observation enable us to perceive patterns and meaning in the world around us, to recognize and interpret the outer, physical aspects as well as the inner world—that mental landscape that helps inform who we are and what we feel and believe. In this book you'll focus on both the exterior and the interior landscapes, particularly as these have been experienced or imagined by writers and as you will express them through your own writing and projects.

We've designed projects that involve you in fieldwork of one kind or another and have selected literature that focuses on the theme of landscapes. We'll ask you to write poems, stories, essays, and scripts as ways of adding various angles of vision to what you already know and believe about both the geographic and societal landscapes of which we are a part. We hope it will be impossible for you to work through this book without reassessing your relationship with the world around you. In what follows, we detail some of our beliefs so that you can get an idea of why we'll ask you to do some of the activities and projects that we do.

Reading means more than opening a book, moving your eyes across a page, and trying to figure out what the author means. *Reading,* as we use the word, involves using all of your knowledge and experience as you work out interpretations of a story, poem, play, or essay. There are many ways to read a book, just as there are many ways to read the world. Reading involves more than understanding words: We talk about reading the weather, reading other people's moods, reading a friend's actions or a parent's tone of voice. If you find various angles from which to read a text, you'll find multiple ways of understanding it.

We use the word *text* often throughout this book, and for us, text means a poem, play, novel, short story, diary entry, essay, letter, film, drawing, painting—nearly anything that requires reading. Text is an artifact of imagining and crafting, something you or someone else creates. The text is like a fabric of many colors or textures with each reader taking a different thread or color of meaning from what's said and not said. In this book, we'll introduce ways that you can step back from the words of a text and look through a variety of lenses and from different angles. Each lens and angle will give you different ways of thinking about the reading.

Other people will read a text differently from the ways you read it. That's one reason we ask you to respond to what you read and then to share your ideas and collaborate with other readers to make comparisons. You will need to listen carefully to one another and be sensitive to why and how your meanings differ. Your experiences with family and friends or in your school or community will influence how you sort through and make sense of the experiences you find in literature. For example, if you've just experienced the death of a close friend, you might respond deeply to a story about death. In short, pay attention. Listen. Question. Keep an open mind. Share your thinking with others. Your class is a community of readers, and it is important to hear different opinions. Remember that while there is no "right" interpretation, you do need to validate your interpretation. It must make sense in light of the text itself, and it must make sense to you, given your own experiences and knowledge. The meaning of what you read is what happens between you, the community of readers, and the text.

We'll also ask you to do many different writing assignments and projects. You'll have experiences as a naturalist and ethnographer as you record close observations and extend those observations into understanding the world around you. We'll ask you to write about your own experiences with the environment and cultures as well as about how authors, including other student writers, report their experiences—from the very smallest of observations to critiques of how we are preparing for our future on this planet. We believe that these assignments are ways for you to think about the topics that other writers raise, to discover your own visions, and to share what you discover with others. We'll ask you to work in multiple ways: record initial reactions; sketch or map ideas; compile field notes; photograph, film, or perform scenes; and write original literature. In activities such as "logs" and "collaborating," we offer choices, which are bulleted, and steps, which are numbered. Some activities will be more useful if you complete all of the steps; in other cases, you are free to choose one or more options. We believe that writing finished pieces takes time and careful attention, so you'll be asked to select some of the assignments that you think hold the most promise and work with your classmates and teacher to revise these into the best possible pieces that you can.

As you work on the projects in this book, you will also explore different ways of seeing, what we call *angles of vision*. Looking at a text from a number of different angles, you'll find multiple ways of understanding it. What are these angles of vision? You might write or draw how you feel after you finish a story or poem; you might tell the story to someone who hasn't read it; you might tell your group about an experience of your own that was similar to what you read and listen to their experiences; or you might write a poem or story of your own. You might read more stories or poems by the same author, or you might reread the story or poem. All of these re-sponses will help you come to your understanding of a text. The an-gles we suggest are not the only ways of looking at a text; there are many others that you'll find by yourself or with your discussion group. We won't be asking you to explore all of these angles for every text that you read, but we will always ask you to look at the text from more than one angle.

Terms and Concepts You Need to Know

Following are some of the terms and concepts that we use fre-quently throughout this book:

Log: The log is where you'll record ongoing work for a particular project. The log may include responses to or discussions about the texts you read. It may include specific observation assignments or lists generated from brainstorming. The form should fit the pur-poses for using the log. Your teacher may prefer one kind of log, such as a loose-leaf notebook; other teachers may prefer spiral notebooks.

In this book, we have numbered the log entries by chapter. When you begin a new chapter, label the new set of log entries with the name of that chapter and begin numbering again with Log Entry 1.

Double-entry Log: There will be some times that we will ask you to set up your log as a double-entry notebook (sometimes called a dual-entry notebook), recording on the left-hand side of the page the words, phrases, or lines that trigger a response for you. On the right-hand side, write your own thoughts and ideas. Set up your log this way:

Double-entry Log Format

Class _____	Name _____
Date _____	Log Entry # _____
Words, phrases, or lines from the text	*My response to the text*

Clustering: Clustering is a process that helps you generate ideas and explore possibilities for writing. Begin by writing the key or stimulus word in the center of a page. Then, in two or three minutes, write as many words and phrases as you can, radiating outward from the key word. Each word or phrase triggers another until you have a web of words and phrases. Usually you find, as you are clustering, that ideas you were not even aware of emerge from the web.

Mapping: Mapping is a more consciously organized way of arranging your ideas on a page than clustering. In mapping, you begin with some ideas or categories and place your items of information meaningfully on the page. The way you organize your material makes it available to you visually. Notes that would take pages, for example, can all be placed on a one-page map. Maps may be completely made up of words; they may use words and symbols or drawings; or they may be completely nonverbal—all symbols and drawings.

Graphic: A graphic is a drawing, cluster, or map. We'll often ask you to respond to or interpret a piece of literature by drawing or mapping your ideas.

Partner or Group: Throughout the book, we will frequently ask you to collaborate with a partner or a small group of your classmates as you explore your understanding of a text and work through revisions in your own writing or performing. Your teacher will establish these groups; they may change from time to time, depending on how your teacher organizes the class.

Writing Folder: The writing folder is a place to keep your work in progress—drafts of essays, stories, and poems. When you work through a particular assignment—writing a draft, having your writing group respond to it and, possibly, revising it—you will keep all of that work in your writing folder.

Course Portfolio: The portfolio represents your best completed work. When you have a finished piece of work, one that your teacher has read and responded to and that you have revised and edited, put that piece into your portfolio. Throughout this book, we suggest many activities that could lead to finished portfolio pieces. Each is identified in the text as a *portfolio entry*.

Angles of Vision on a Poem

To demonstrate how various readings and perspectives can contribute to the meanings we make from text, we ask you now to read from seven different angles of vision the poem "Traveling Through the Dark." Because we want you to respond first to the poem itself, we omit the poet's name until the fourth angle.

Remember that this is practice, to acquaint you with the strategies you will develop as you read and write your way through *Learning the Landscape*. To work through these angles, you will need to set up a log. Your teacher will explain how you are to establish partners for sharing and collaborating. Begin by reading the poem; then follow directions for each of the seven angles of vision. You will not have to read other works this many times, but we hope experimenting with these seven angles of vision will help you explore possibilities for how to read other selections in this book.

Angle 1: Initial Responses

Traveling Through the Dark

Traveling through the dark I found a deer
dead on the edge of the Wilson River road.
It is usually best to roll them into the canyon:
that road is narrow; to swerve might make more dead.

By glow of the tail-light I stumbled back of the car
and stood by the heap, a doe, a recent killing;
she had stiffened already, almost cold.
I dragged her off; she was large in the belly.

My fingers touching her side brought me the reason—
her side was warm; her fawn lay there waiting,
alive, still, never to be born.
Beside that mountain road I hesitated.

The car aimed ahead its lowered parking lights;
under the hood purred the steady engine.
I stood in the glare of the warm exhaust turning red;
around our group I could hear the wilderness listen.

I thought hard for us all—my only swerving—,
then pushed her over the edge into the river.

Log Entry 1

After reading this poem, what are your initial thoughts, feelings, observations, questions? You may express them in pictures as well as words.

Angle 2: Story Threads

Traveling Through the Dark

Traveling through the dark I found a deer
dead on the edge of the Wilson River road.
It is usually best to roll them into the canyon:
that road is narrow; to swerve might make more dead.

By glow of the tail-light I stumbled back of the car
and stood by the heap, a doe, a recent killing;
she had stiffened already, almost cold.
I dragged her off; she was large in the belly.

My fingers touching her side brought me the reason—
her side was warm; her fawn lay there waiting,

alive, still, never to be born.
Beside that mountain road I hesitated.

The car aimed ahead its lowered parking lights;
under the hood purred the steady engine.
I stood in the glare of the warm exhaust turning red;
around our group I could hear the wilderness listen.

I thought hard for us all—my only swerving—,
then pushed her over the edge into the river.

Collaborating

With your partner, share stories about "traveling through the dark."
Have you had or do you know of experiences similar to the ones the
poet describes? Your stories needn't be about actual darkness; they
could also be about times you had to make a decision or came upon
something unexpectedly. Whatever the experience, think about
what you noticed. What did you feel? Your stories can be your personal experiences, or they can be experiences you've heard or read
about.

Log Entry 2

Record in pictures and/or words the similarities, or common
threads, in all the stories you've told and heard.

Angle 3: Shifting Perspectives

Traveling Through the Dark

Traveling through the dark I found a deer
dead on the edge of the Wilson River road.
It is usually best to roll them into the canyon:
that road is narrow; to swerve might make more dead.

By glow of the tail-light I stumbled back of the car
and stood by the heap, a doe, a recent killing;
she had stiffened already, almost cold.
I dragged her off; she was large in the belly.

My fingers touching her side brought me the reason—
her side was warm; her fawn lay there waiting,
alive, still, never to be born.
Beside that mountain road I hesitated.

The car aimed ahead its lowered parking lights;
under the hood purred the steady engine.
I stood in the glare of the warm exhaust turning red;
around our group I could hear the wilderness listen.

I thought hard for us all—my only swerving—,
then pushed her over the edge into the river.

Collaborating

Speculate with your partner on how you might read this poem differently if

- you were totally unfamiliar with surroundings such as these.
- you have had an unpleasant experience that this poem makes you recall.
- you believe the speaker of the poem is an elderly man.
- you believe the speaker of the poem is a teenager.
- you believe the speaker of the poem is a pregnant woman.

Log Entry 3

Record a summary of your discussion.

Angle 4: Connecting with the Writer

Poet of "Traveling Through the Dark," William Stafford, was born in 1914 in Hutchinson, Kansas, and was raised in small towns on the Kansas plains. He was a conscientious objector who worked in civilian public service camps during World War II. Although he taught elsewhere for short periods of time, he spent most of his career at Lewis and Clark College in Portland, Oregon. He died in 1993.

He often spoke or wrote about his craft. In *An Oregon Message,* Stafford said: "Each poem is a miracle that has been invited to happen" (Harper & Row, 1987, p. 10). Stafford believed that a poem was more than its subject as well. He wrote, "A poem is anything said in such a way or put on the page in such a way as to invite from the hearer or reader a certain kind of attention" (*Writing the Australian Crawl,* University of Michigan Press, 1978, p. 61). For Stafford, a poem was a kind of performance.

In light of your knowledge about the poet, read the following poems, also by William Stafford:

Ask Me

Some time when the river is ice ask me
mistakes I have made. Ask me whether
what I have done is my life. Others
have come in their slow way into
my thought, and some have tried to help
or to hurt: ask me what difference
their strongest love or hate has made.

I will listen to what you say.
You and I can turn and look
at the silent river and wait. We know
the current is there, hidden; and there
are comings and goings from miles away
that hold the stillness exactly before us.
What the river says, that is what I say.

To You Around Me

The ways I follow go down by the river
and look out. They pause on the pavement by a church
where a stone says, "Old." They take me slowly

to a house behind a white gate, still,
and clean, and vacant. The ways I follow
won't rest. They find the country and cross
a field where a killdeer is grieving for its mate.
Evening begins to move near. Something
calls through the stars, telling me
to be brave and also be afraid.
You around me, is it like this for you?—
far, full of surprises, lonely
and scary sometimes, on the ways you follow?

Collaborating

- Talk with your partner about how knowing details from the poet's life affects your reading of "Traveling Through the Dark."

- Discuss with your partner how knowing what Stafford says about writing poems affects your reading. *Do* the poems "invite . . . a certain kind of attention"?

- Describe how your reading of these two poems by William Stafford affects your reading of "Traveling Through the Dark."

Log Entry 4

Record a brief summary of your discussion.

Angle 5: Language and Craft

Traveling Through the Dark
William Stafford

Traveling through the dark I found a deer
dead on the edge of the Wilson River road.
It is usually best to roll them into the canyon:
that road is narrow; to swerve might make more dead.

By glow of the tail-light I stumbled back of the car
and stood by the heap, a doe, a recent killing;
she had stiffened already, almost cold.
I dragged her off; she was large in the belly.

My fingers touching her side brought me the reason—
her side was warm; her fawn lay there waiting,
alive, still, never to be born.
Beside that mountain road I hesitated.

The car aimed ahead its lowered parking lights;
under the hood purred the steady engine.
I stood in the glare of the warm exhaust turning red;
around our group I could hear the wilderness listen.

I thought hard for us all—my only swerving—,
then pushed her over the edge into the river.

*Lo*g Entry 5

Use the double-entry log format, and in the left column jot down
words and phrases from the poem that catch your attention or that
are particularly interesting to you. In the right column, write a brief
explanation of why you chose the words and phrases you did.

*Co*llaborating

- Discuss with your partner the choices you made and why you selected each one. Are the phrases you selected ones that you like
  because of images or sounds or because of the ways in which
  they make you feel or see? What other reasons?

- How does the title, "Traveling Through the Dark," contribute to
  the meaning you make from the poem? Is the traveling literal or
  metaphorical or both? If you were to give the poem a new title,
  what would it be and why?

Angle 6: Recasting the Poem

Traveling Through the Dark
William Stafford

Traveling through the dark I found a deer
dead on the edge of the Wilson River road.
It is usually best to roll them into the canyon:
that road is narrow; to swerve might make more dead.

By glow of the tail-light I stumbled back of the car
and stood by the heap, a doe, a recent killing;
she had stiffened already, almost cold.
I dragged her off; she was large in the belly.

My fingers touching her side brought me the reason—
her side was warm; her fawn lay there waiting,
alive, still, never to be born.
Beside that mountain road I hesitated.

The car aimed ahead its lowered parking lights;
under the hood purred the steady engine.
I stood in the glare of the warm exhaust turning red;
around our group I could hear the wilderness listen.

I thought hard for us all—my only swerving—,
then pushed her over the edge into the river.

*L*og Entry 6

Try your hand at recasting this poem in any of the following ways
or in a way of your own.

- Draw what the poem means to you.

- Bring to class an object that represents what the poem means to
  you and explain the connections.

- Write the poem as a brief story, dialogue, or scene. You may
  want to read what you have written aloud or act it out for the
  class or a small group.

Angle 7: You, the Text, the World

Traveling Through the Dark
William Stafford

Traveling through the dark I found a deer
dead on the edge of the Wilson River road.
It is usually best to roll them into the canyon:
that road is narrow; to swerve might make more dead.

By glow of the tail-light I stumbled back of the car
and stood by the heap, a doe, a recent killing;
she had stiffened already, almost cold.
I dragged her off; she was large in the belly.

My fingers touching her side brought me the reason—
her side was warm; her fawn lay there waiting,
alive, still, never to be born.
Beside that mountain road I hesitated.

The car aimed ahead its lowered parking lights;
under the hood purred the steady engine.
I stood in the glare of the warm exhaust turning red;
around our group I could hear the wilderness listen.

I thought hard for us all—my only swerving—,
then pushed her over the edge into the river.

*Lo*g Entry 7

- Read through your log entries and review your various readings of this poem.

- Trace how your understanding or appreciation of the poem has changed by creating a visual map depicting the changes. Or write a description of how your reading changed as you talked, wrote, drew, and read this poem from various angles of vision.

- Create your own structure for connecting you, the text, and the world.

Building Your Course Portfolio

Periodically, as you work through this book, we will suggest that you compose a piece for your portfolio. While your writing folder contains notes, first drafts, and short pieces written without extensive revision, your *course portfolio* is a collection of finished works that represents your best thinking about an idea or works of literature you have been studying. Your portfolio pieces may include a piece of writing, a graphic, a live performance, a video presentation, or some combination. For the graphic, video presentation, and oral performance options, which probably will not fit into a portfolio, include a photograph or a carefully written description of your work, along with notes, scripts, or tapes. In this book we frequently identify possible portfolio pieces as a *portfolio entry*.

Usually the portfolio work will come after you have read a number of related texts. In this introductory section, however, which acquaints you with techniques that you will use throughout the book, your first portfolio piece will be in response to the Stafford poem "Traveling Through the Dark."

Portfolio Entry

The following is the process for building your portfolio entry:

1. Reread the logs you wrote about the Stafford poem for each of the angles of vision.

2. Think about the ideas you would like to work with for your portfolio entry.

3. Once you have tentatively decided on an idea, do some clustering or brainstorming to generate additional ideas.

As you worked through the various approaches to this one poem, you

• recorded your thoughts and feelings.

• looked at parallel stories from previous reading you have done or experiences you have had.

- speculated on how your reading might be different if you had changed various aspects of the poem.

- noted how additional information about Stafford affected your reading.

- recorded words and phrases you liked and explored reasons for your choices.

- recast the poem in different ways.

- reflected on how your understanding or appreciation changed as you worked through the various angles of vision.

Content and Form

You will need to consider two aspects of your product: the *nature* of the idea you want to develop, and the *form* or *forms* you want to use to develop that idea. Each will affect the other. Following are some options, but don't feel limited by these. You may want to think of some of your own options.

Written options
- an original poem based on an experience you have had

- a written dialogue based on your logs for Angle 3: Shifting Perspectives

- a story based loosely on a real-life experience you have had or know about, one that has similarities to the experience of the speaker of the poem

- a paper about William Stafford, based on additional readings of his poetry and information about his life

- a story based on the information of the poem but with an alternative ending. What if, for example, the man had been able to save the fawn's life?

Graphic options
You probably have the origin of an idea for a graphic in your logs. Look through them for ideas about how you might present your

thoughts on the work in this chapter. Graphic options can stand alone or accompany a written option. If the graphic stands alone, write a short explanation of your use of symbols and colors for your portfolio.

For graphics, try to use good quality paper. You will need marking pens, crayons, or watercolors. You do not need artistic ability to begin working with graphics; your goal is to translate your ideas into symbols and images, using both drawings and words as they are appropriate. You are not simply illustrating the work; you are showing how you understand the work through color, symbol, shape, line, or texture. Here are some suggestions that may stimulate some ideas:

- Map the events of the poem.

- Design a graphic presentation of the story of the poem.

- Think of symbols to represent the speaker, the idea of the poem, the doe, or the journey. Draw these symbols in a way that shows their relationships to each other.

Performance options

Performance options may include written work and graphics as well as performances, if they are part of the presentation. You may want to work with a partner or in a small group to prepare a dramatic performance. You may, of course, design a solo presentation. Following are some suggestions:

- Look closely at your log entries for Angle 6. Working with a partner, write out and refine one of the suggested dialogues or one of your own. Present your dialogue to a larger group or to the class.

- Look back at the logs you have written for Angles 2, 3, and 6. Working with two or three classmates, prepare a storytelling session, with all of the stories dealing in some way with the relationship between a person and an animal. Refine your storytelling by listening to each other and making suggestions. Decide which order works best for your stories. Then present your stories to the class.

- Reread the Stafford poem. With a partner serving as a director, plan "freeze frames" for significant points in the poem. Plan how you will physically represent the speaker at each point. What facial expressions? What gestures? What stance—standing, kneeling, bending over? Using the director's suggestions, polish your performance for the class. The director will read the poem aloud as you present your interpretation and move from frame to frame.

From Process to Product

The success of your final product—written, graphic, oral, or a combination—depends on your ability to see something through to completion. There are several factors that will help you learn how you work best and how you can take advantage of that knowledge as you develop an idea into its best possible form.

The following steps in working through a major paper or project will help you present your ideas in their best possible form.

1. Messing around
You need to be able to tolerate the "messing around" stage. Often this stage will begin in your journal or log entries. To find out exactly what you want to do, however, you need to be able to make a number of starts, often in different directions. You can explore your own best way to get started by trying out different strategies such as clustering, mapping, listing, or brainstorming. Each of these suggestions will be explored as we go along in this book.

2. Making a rough draft, notes, and sketches
Once you have decided on your idea, you need to cultivate your own space in which to write or draw. In your first draft, try to develop your ideas as fully as you can in a short period of time. Once you have your ideas roughly sketched out, you can begin the revising process, seeing the work and your ideas anew. Throughout the book, we have included many ideas to show you how to turn a rough draft into a finished product you can be proud of.

3. Collaborating
We cannot stress enough the value of collaboration once you have a rough draft of your first ideas. This is the time for response groups, for sharing your work and getting feedback from others. Because you are the one who knows what your goal is, you are the one who

must tell your partners what you need from them. Sometimes you may want just to have them listen; other times you may want specific suggestions for revising your work. From time to time, we present specific response-group suggestions and guidelines. For now, use your best understanding of what you need from your group, and be sure to give back to the others what they ask of you.

4. Revising

Again, after the collaboration, you will need a quiet time for further revision and refinement. Regardless of the help others may offer, each word or placement of design is ultimately your decision; you will take both the praise and the criticism. This part of the process is often the most satisfying, when you see your work really taking shape and becoming more than you even dreamed of in the beginning.

5. Editing

With written work, this is the final step before publication. At this stage you may need the help of a partner, or you may need to consult a dictionary or writing handbook. If you are using a word processor, be sure to use the spell check, but remember that it does not catch certain kinds of typographical errors (*on* for *one,* for example). You need to proofread carefully and, if possible, get someone else to proofread for you (not because you wouldn't recognize a typo, but because your eyes see what your brain expects.)

6. Publishing

This is the next-to-the-last step. For classroom projects, publication can take many different forms. Finished written projects go into your course portfolio, the collection of works you consider ready for publication. Finished graphics should be accompanied by a presentation to the class and be displayed on the wall of the classroom. Finished performances can be presented to other classes as well as your own. Several of you may plan to take your performance "on the road," presenting it for your school open house, a PTA meeting, or an elementary school assembly. (Our students say that children are often the best audiences.) For finished work that cannot go into the portfolio, write a short, concise explanation of the graphic or oral performance that you created for your project. Include the chapter title, the assignment that you chose or your teacher gave you, and a description of the finished work.

7. Evaluating

Although your teacher will evaluate both your finished product and your work throughout the process, your own evaluation is an important key to your growth as a self-sufficient reader, writer, and performer. It is important to step back and reflect on your accomplishments. Before you can do that usefully, you need to think through what your goals were in the beginning, how they changed as you worked, and how your final product reflects your thinking. Your teacher may provide specific suggestions for self-assessment throughout the chapters. For now, try writing a very short assessment of your final product for this one chapter. In it, state what you hoped to accomplish when you began and how your final work measures up to or exceeds your expectations.

As your portfolio grows, you will be able to trace the record of your best work. At the end of the course, you will have a substantial body of your own work to serve as a record of your growth as a reader, writer, graphic artist, and performer.

2

Ways of Seeing: From Observation to Reflection

*T*his chapter focuses on helping you learn to see and to pay attention to what you see. One goal is to help you become a more discerning "reader"—of the world around you as well as of books. Another goal is to help you develop or fine-tune your senses, using the techniques of biologists and botanists in the field. You will gain practice in observing and reflecting as you record your impressions of what you see and translate those observations into words. The logs, poems, and essays you write will convey your particular view of the world to others.

The field notes work will guide you as you record your observations, use research to supplement your own vision, map your data, and reflect on and write about your experience. Layered into the field-work are poems, essays, dialogues, and letters, as well as opportunities to enhance your seeing through drawing, talking, and writing. These activities are designed to help you think about your ability to see through your own and others' minds and eyes. We hope that you will come to a deeper understanding of the many aspects of vision— from the physical sense of *eye-sight* to the mental set of *in-sight,* which actually enables you to make meaning of what you see.

Literature selections range from those by well-known authors— Henry David Thoreau, Helen Keller, and John Steinbeck—to works of lesser-known poet/naturalists or naturalist/poets. You will examine writing by other students. Some of the pieces are grouped in order to show different perspectives of similar experiences.

Here are a few specifics that are important in this chapter:

1. You will need to keep all of your work—log entries, drawings, and drafts—in a writing folder.

2. Groups will work together to discuss literature, explore options in writing, help each other with the re-visioning process, and serve as a supportive audience for finished work.

3. You may decide to include several finished pieces from this chapter in your course portfolio.

*P*erception

Thoreau was right when he wrote in *Walden*: "There is no power to see in the eye itself, any more than there is in any other jelly." Yet it is through the eye that we receive the electromagnetic band of energy that allows our minds to construct meaning from marks on the page. "I'll believe it when I see it," the saying goes, but what happens when you turn that phrase around? "I'll see it when I believe it!" Seeing, as you will discover from your work in this chapter, is not all in the eyes. Look, for example, at the following arrangement of numbers and letters:

$$\begin{matrix} & A & \\ 12 & 13 & 14 \\ & C & \end{matrix}$$

How did you first read the character in the middle? Did your perception change as you looked at it longer? Look at it again. What is it now? Does it keep changing?

Our minds have the power to transform the character in the middle from a "B" to a "13" and back again as we make sense of the arrangement of impressions that bombard our retinas. When we use the word *see,* then, we generally mean more than what the eye can do; we mean what we do, with our personal backlogs of experience, our own preconceptions, our own histories. The eye receives impressions; we see.

Scientists and artists have been experimenting with optical illusions for years, trying to understand how the eye can fool us into seeing something different from what can be proved. Here are some examples of such illusions, all taken from the book *Science, Art, and Visual Illusions* by Robert Froman (Simon and Schuster, 1970, pp. 48, 49, 50, 89, 90, 91):

> If two lines of equal length interrupt each other at their centers, most people experience no illusion:

But if the lines interrupt each other unequally, the illusion crops up again—the line with the greater uninterrupted stretch seeming longer than the other:

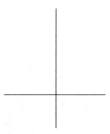

The illusion disappears again when the interruption again is equalized:

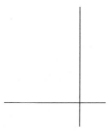

Another visual illusion, discovered in 1889 by a German psychologist, Franz Muller-Lyer, has led to a wide variety of hypotheses:

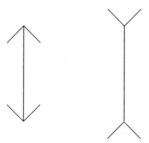

The illusion that the vertical line on the right is longer than the one on the left is so strong that you probably will have to measure with a ruler to persuade yourself that the two are of the same length. Muller-Lyer and other research workers showed drawings like this to many people, all of whom found it hard to believe that the lines were equal.

A number of other illusions involving arrows also have been studied. For example:

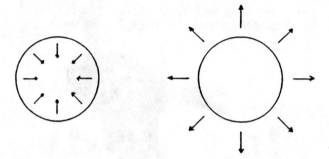

Almost everyone who sees these drawings thinks the circle with the outward-pointing arrows around it is bigger than the one with inward-pointing arrows inside it. One hypothesis is that the arrows direct attention in a way that makes one circle seem to expand and the other to contract. A similar effect seems to occur with other figures.

Here is the effect on equal squares:

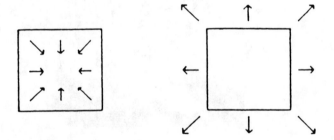

And here is the effect on equilateral triangles:

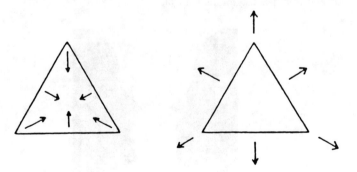

It is not only with geometrical figures that this sort of thing happens. Complex drawings depicting familiar things also can present
contradictory information, causing us to construct first one image
and then another quite different one. One of the oldest and best-
known examples is the duck-or-rabbit drawing:

Still more complicated and more startling when you first switch
from one visual image to another is a drawing sometimes called
Daisy or the Duchess:

A slightly different kind of drawing offering two sets of information is the sort in which the viewer must decide what is foreground
and what is background. For example:

If you take the white space to be the foreground, you construct a visual image of a wide-topped vase. If you take the black space as the foreground, you construct an image of two human profiles facing each other.

But the most interesting drawings of this sort are the so-called "impossible" ones. For example:

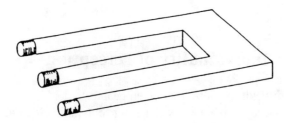

Many people report that looking at this figure for any length of time makes them feel uncomfortable, in some cases even dizzy. There is, obviously, an important difference between this drawing and the others we have been considering.

In the case of the vase-or-profiles drawing, for instance, one can make a choice between two sets of information. One can concentrate on the set of information that makes it possible to construct a visual image of a white vase against a black background. Or one can concentrate on the set that makes it possible to construct an image of black profiles facing each other across a white background. What makes the new drawing "impossible" is that the two contradictory sets of information are so thoroughly blended with each other that it is difficult to separate them and attend to one while ignoring the other.

Informing the eye is a way of talking about how we actually perceive the world and how we can use our minds to make sense of the billions of images our retinas receive every second. Even though Thoreau was right, in a scientific sense, we will use the word *eye* the way people do when they say such things as, "He has a good eye for a fastball," or "Keep an eye out for a gas station. We're running on empty."

*Co*llaborating

Take a few minutes to list common English phrases that use the word *eye* to mean the act of seeing. Then check with others to see what phrases they came up with. (An unabridged dictionary will give you a lengthy list under the heading "eye.")

The point of generating such a list is to see how the eye, the organ that permits us to see, permeates our language. Try the same exercise with the other sense organs—the ear, the nose, the tongue, the skin—and see whether they are reflected as strongly in the idioms of English.

The Individuality of Perception

It's difficult to realize that when people are looking at the same thing, they are, in fact, each seeing something different. We know that to be true intellectually. We have all experienced some variation of listening to three different eye-witnesses describe an incident, but most of us find it hard to know what "really" happened. The instant replay that television football viewers have become accustomed to has now become a formal part of officiating. What one official sees is not necessarily what another sees. The coach who storms up and down the sidelines shouting his version of a play knows he is right. The official knows otherwise. Even the players involved in a controversial call give different versions; each of them is "right." Who is to say? Is the television camera able to see all angles at once? Does instant replay solve the problem of what "really" happened? Do multiple angles come closer to what we call *objectivity?*

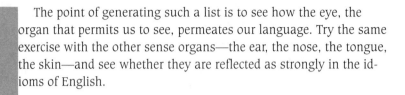

*Lo*g Entry 1

Jot down your perceptions of your classroom. Just write what you see. Share your log with two or three other students and compare versions. Here are a few questions to consider:

- What particular things in the room did you focus on? Did you and your discussion partners describe any of the same things? If so, compare your descriptions.

- Did you focus on the people in the room? Other students? Your teacher?

- Did your journal entry express your feelings about specific objects in the room or about the room itself?

- Did you include color in your description? Did you and others include any of the same colors?

Most of us take our perception of color for granted. White is white; we don't need to define it. Naomi Shihab Nye has something to say about defining white in her poem of the same name.

Defining White

Naomi Shihab Nye

On the telephone no one knows what white is.
My husband knows, he takes pictures.
He has whole notebooks defining
how white is white, is black,
and all the gray neighborhoods in between.

The telephone is blind.
Cream-white? Off-white?
I want a white, we say,
that is white-white,
that tends in no direction
other than itself.

Now this is getting complex.
Every white I see is tending
toward something else.
The house was white, but it is peeling.
People are none of these colors.

In the sky white sentences form and detach.
Who speaks here? What breath
scrawls itself endlessly,
white on white, without being heard?
Is wind a noun or a verb?

Log Entry 2

Write your response to "Defining White" in your journal. What images does it create for you? What thoughts? In what ways is it a poem about color? About ideas?

Careful observers pay particular attention to color, exploring how color affects our moods and speculating about whether what we call *blue,* for example, appears the same to different people. A contemporary artist, Lynn Lonidier, gives us this suggestion: Go to a paint store and ask for a sample color chart for any brand of paint. Take any strip of colors and observe the subtle differences as your eye moves from one to another. Are there any that look the same to you?

- If you have a numbered chart, try giving each paint sample an appropriate name, one that clearly distinguishes it from the ones directly above or below.

- If your chart already has names, do you find them descriptive? Can you tell whether the words influenced you to see the color you did? Try changing the names.

Lynn Lonidier constructed a mock paint chart using color chips that were all the same color but giving each chip a distinctive name. The observer, because of the power of the different names, found it difficult to believe that the chips were all one color. You might try this yourself to test the power of the mind on what we think of as vision.

Work in Progress

Choose one of the writing possibilities that follow to draft a piece for your writing folder. You may decide to revise and edit it later for inclusion in your portfolio.

- Select a color that interests you and write a sustained prose exploration of the impact that color has on you.

- Write a poem entitled "Defining _____," whatever color you find interesting. You might want to reread "Defining White" before you begin, although you don't need to follow Nye's pattern in your own poem.

- Consider the clothes and hairstyles that are in fashion today. How would the way your parents describe your clothes differ from the way you would?

- Think about all of the cars and trucks you see on streets and freeways. Describe the one that you like best—either one that you own or one that you would like to own. Then think of someone you know who wouldn't appreciate that car or truck at all, someone who would describe it very differently. Describe it as it must appear to that other person.

- Choose another subject to describe from two points of view. You might even write a dialogue, with two people discussing or arguing about the appearance of the object.

Extending the Boundaries of Perception

You may have discovered that people often make assumptions about how something looks without really noticing its distinguishing details. The psychologist William James observed that our senses not only permit us to know objects in the world around us, but they also serve as a filter or fuse, to prevent us from sensory overload. Most of the time, we see what we expect to see. Unless we stop and really look, however, we will never extend the boundaries of what we expect to see.

Careful observation is a habit of mind, one that can be altered by direct training. The activities suggested here are adapted from methods used by naturalists, people who study plants and animals in their natural habitats or settings. Naturalists talk of going into the field to study their subjects; the "field" is wherever they can find their subjects. The notes they take in the field they call, appropriately, *field notes*.

Field Notes

To get an idea of how naturalists in the field actually work, read the following recorded dialogue between Ann Zwinger and Gary Nabhan (from "Field Notes and the Literary Process," *Writing Natural History,* University of Utah Press, 1989, pp. 78-80). They were comparing notes at a writing seminar about how they record their field observations.

Zwinger, nature writer and illustrator, said, "When you take field notes, there are a lot of devices that I think you use to observe well. I certainly sketch in the margin of the page, which provides a wonderful backup. You consciously call on all six senses; you have a way of ticking them off in your mind: What does it smell like? What does it look like?"

Nabhan, botanical researcher and writer, seemed to understand what Zwinger meant when she reported calling on all "six senses." Most scientists acknowledge that we possess more than the traditional five senses—sight, sound, taste, touch, smell; we lump all of the senses that we don't understand into the catch phrase "the sixth sense." Although some people may use the term to refer to some kind of telepathy, scientists believe that eventually we will understand and be able to identify a number of additional ways of knowing.

Nabhan responded to Zwinger's comments with, "Well, I depend upon all senses when I'm out there. Unless I do, when I get back to a cozy room with my notebook . . . I won't be able to remember the sounds that were there, or what the light was like. When I take a lot of notes in the field, there is a chance that some of the sounds I hear in that landscape will carry over into the sounds of the words I use to describe a place. I work hard on that because I can't do that again later. Recording the weather is also important. I feel I have failed when I read a journal entry and I can't even tell whether it was raining on me at the time other than that the ink is smeared . . . "

To which Ann Zwinger retorted, "That's why I use a pencil."

"It's the sensory data that I want to record in detail," Nabhan continued.

"It's strange that so many people nowadays depend on a camera or a tape recorder . . . ; it doesn't altogether serve, does it? You have

BUSINESS REPLY MAIL

FIRST-CLASS MAIL   PERMIT NO. 1338   BOULDER CO

POSTAGE WILL BE PAID BY ADDRESSEE

Newsweek

PO BOX 59927
BOULDER CO 80323-9927

to find some salient feature which comes through the other senses, or a combination of the senses. One of the things in that boiling down is olfactory—the sense of smell, which is so often left out of our recounting of experience."

Zwinger agreed: "You know, our sense of smell is a very primitive sense. Do you realize the only way you can describe smells is to say it smells *like?* There is no precise primary vocabulary. . . . I've just sweated blood trying to describe the odors of desert plants."

"That's why we call it the hot, stinking desert," said Nabhan.

It is not surprising to find that many naturalists move from recording stark, scientific field notes to writing personal essays, journals, and poems. In the field, a scientist attempts to be objective, to record only what is "out there," yet as Nabhan and Zwinger show us, their perceptions of light, weather, and smell all figure strongly into their scientific field notes.

The scientist Werner Karl Heisenberg gave voice to what naturalists and poets had long known—that what is "out there" is determined by what is "in here." Heisenberg's principle, which has had an enormous effect on how scientists perceive experiments and observations, states that what is observed is affected by the observer. This theory, which underlies the belief in the interrelatedness of all aspects of our world, affects the entire idea of being able to look at something objectively. If the person looking affects the thing being looked at, then two persons observing the same object or phenomenon will end up with different descriptions. We know from our own experience that this kind of disparity is what happens in the real world (remember the instant replay). You will be asked to draw on this knowledge in the activities that follow. In order to "inform the eye," then, we will use Heisenberg's discovery and trust our own participation in the observation as we draw on the experience of practiced naturalists and writers.

Preparation for Going Out into the Field

The first part of your venture in this background training unit to help "inform the eye" is to emulate the naturalists who go into the field to examine plants and animals in their own habitat. The field, of course, can be any place at all; *field* is the term for the place where the object of study can be found in its natural state. A school classroom might be the "field" for studying that species known as "second-semester junior." For this first study, however, you will actually go out into a place where you can observe an animal or plant in its natural habitat. Interspersed with your own field study will be short statements from naturalists and poets, whose eyes are well informed. As you progress through this workshop in "informing your eye," you will have opportunities to engage in many different ways of coming to know the object you choose to study. You will observe, draw, compare, read other people's poems and essays, talk, reflect, and write.

You are also going to record the factors "in here" (that is, in yourself) that alter your perceptions of what is "out there." You will need some kind of notebook and, if you follow Ann Zwinger's suggestion, a pencil, in case of rain.

Selecting Your Subject

Select the subject for your field notes study—an animal, plant, or natural object that you can observe over a period of time. If you choose a specific kind of bird—a duck, for example—be sure that you can find a duck to observe over the next few days. Typical selections include a wide range of subjects, from specific trees, flowers, ivy, and weeds to insects, birds, tidepool inhabitants, and four-legged animals. Some students choose to focus on a completely dependable subject such as a shell or rock, while others set up telescopes to observe the moon.

In selecting your subject for observation, keep in mind the following criteria:

- its accessibility over the next few days (Don't forget insects or trees.)

- your ability to sustain interest in your subject (Hard to predict, but try.)

- possibilities for your own reflecting, perhaps making connections between the subject you are observing and the way people behave (The spider and patience, the bee and "busy-ness," the rose and love—these are well worn, but always open to new eyes. Better, though, is making your own connection.)

Firsthand Information: In the Field

Log Entry 3

Observation 1: Firsthand Information

For your first observation, spend about fifteen minutes actually looking at your subject. Pay attention to the details of the subject, but also be aware of your environment and of your own feelings at the time of your observation.

Record the following introductory data as part of your field notes:

Name _____

Date _____

Subject of observation _____

Environment details:

    Location _____

    Weather _____

Time of day _____

Length of time of observation _____

Set up your field notes as a dual-entry notebook, as illustrated below:

Descriptive Notes (the "out there")	Reflective Notes (the "in here")
Suggestions: Include all observed data such as size, movement, behavior, eating habits, color patterns. You may include a sketch or series of sketches of your subject.	Suggestions: Record how you are feeling, what memories or associations the observation triggers, how the weather or time of day affects how you see your subject. These notes may be brief or expansive.

Samples of field notes follow. Debbie Carpenter's logs (Figures 2-1 through 2-5) show how one student worked through the process described in this chapter. A professional's field notes provide yet another perspective or observation.

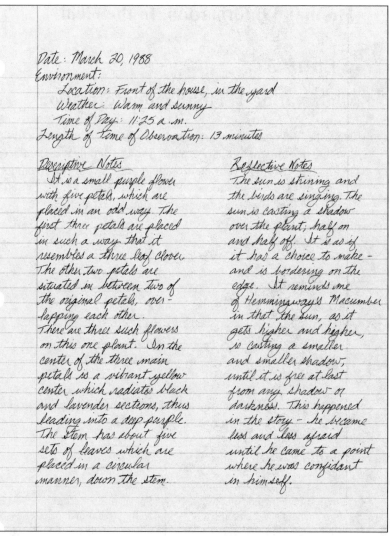

Date: March 20, 1988
Environment:
   Location: Front of the house, in the yard
   Weather: Warm and sunny
   Time of Day: 11:25 a.m.
   Length of time of Observation: 13 minutes

Descriptive Notes

It is a small purple flower with five petals, which are placed in an odd way. The first three petals are placed in such a way that it resembles a three leaf clover. The other two petals are situated in between two of the original petals, overlapping each other. There are three such flowers on this one plant. In the center of the three main petals is a vibrant yellow center which radiates black and lavender sections, thus leading into a deep purple. The stem has about five sets of leaves which are placed in a circular manner, down the stem.

Reflective Notes

The sun is shining and the birds are singing. The sun is casting a shadow over the plant; half on and half off. It is as if it has a choice to make – and is bordering on the edge. It reminds me of Hemmingway's Macumber in that the sun, as it gets higher and higher, is casting a smaller and smaller shadow, until it is free at last from any shadow or darkness. This happened in the story – he became less and less afraid until he came to a point where he was confidant in himself.

Figure 2-1. *Debbie Carpenter's First Log*

Notice that in the following extract from *The Audubon Society Field Guide to North American Birds* (Alfred A. Knopf, 1977), the authors draw from many observations. They make inferences about reasons for robin behavior, using popular culture as a reference for our understanding and making comparisons to common knowledge, as in "fox-red" and "cup-like."

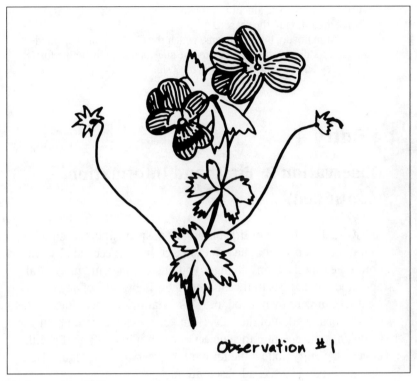

Observation #1

Figure 2-1. *Debbie Carpenter's First Log (continued)*

American Robin

"Robin"

Description: 9" to 11" Perhaps the best known of all North American birds. Puffed-out breast is a *fox-red or orange color*; gray-brown upperparts; throat white, head and tail blackish, paler in the female.

Voice: Many regard the rich caroling of the male, uttered from a high perch, as the true herald of spring. It consists of clear rising and falling phrases recalling the words "cheer-up," "cheerily," etc.

Habitat: Lawns and parks in suburbs; any wooded habitat. Also mountain meadows interspersed with woods.

Nesting: 3 or 4 blue eggs in garden shrubbery or boulevard trees in a cup-like nest of roots and small twigs, reinforced with mud and lined with fine material. Early in spring, when cold threatens the brood, it hides its nest low in densely needled branches of a cedar or a juniper bush. During later broods, when summer heat may prostrate an incubating female, the nest is placed high in a maple or sycamore where leafy branches evaporate moisture and cool the surrounding air. The amount of mud in the insulating wall is also varied according to the season.

Their mainstay is earthworms, which they hunt on lawns, standing stock-still with head cocked to one side as though listening for their prey but actually discovering it by sight.

Log Entry 4

Observation 2: Firsthand Information (continued)

At least a day after your first observation, spend another ten to fifteen minutes observing the same subject. In your second observation, note especially any changes you observe in your subject. Take note, too, of changes in the environment (light, time of day, weather), in your own mood, or in associations or memories evoked by your observation of the subject. In your sketches, you might focus on some detail of the subject or catch it in a different position. In your log entry, follow the format for Observation 1. Figure 2-2 is Debbie Carpenter's second observation.

Close Observation: A Student's View of a Fish

Before going on with your own field notes, read this description of close observation from a memoir written a century ago by Samuel Scudder as he recounted his student days at Harvard studying with Louis Agassiz, a well-known professor of paleontology. Agassiz (1807–1873) required his students to observe their specimens and, when they had exhausted all that they could possibly see, to go back and observe again.

Remembering Agassiz
Samuel Scudder

It was more than fifteen years ago that I entered the laboratory of Professor Agassiz, and told him I had enrolled my name in the Scien-

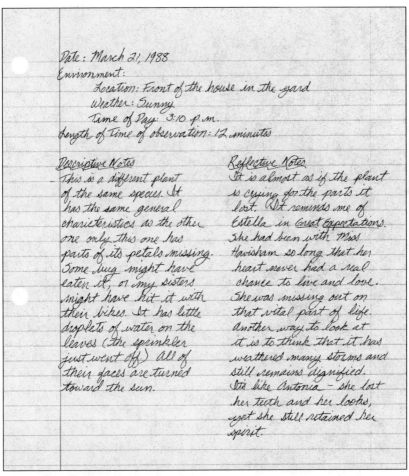

Date: March 21, 1988
Environment:
    Location: Front of the house in the yard
    Weather: Sunny
    Time of Day: 3:10 p.m.
Length of Time of observation: 12 minutes

Descriptive Notes
- This is a different plant of the same species. It has the same general characteristics as the other one only this one has parts of its petals missing. Some bug might have eaten it, or my sisters might have hit it with their bikes. It has little droplets of water on the leaves (the sprinkler just went off) all of their faces are turned toward the sun.

Reflective Notes
It is almost as if the plant is crying for the parts it lost. It reminds me of Estella in Great Expectations. She had been with Miss Havisham so long that her heart never had a real chance to live and love. She was missing out on that vital part of life. Another way to look at it is to think that it has weathered many storms and still remains dignified. Its like Antonia — she lost her teeth and her looks, yet she still retained her spirit.

Figure 2-2. *Debbie Carpenter's Second Log*

tific School as a student of natural history. He asked me a few questions about my object in coming, my antecedents generally, the mode in which I afterwards proposed to use the knowledge I might acquire, and finally, whether I wished to study any special branch. To the latter I replied that, while I wished to be well grounded in all departments of zoology, I purposed to devote myself specially to insects.

"When do you wish to begin?" he asked.

"Now," I replied.

This seemed to please him, and with an energetic "Very well!" he reached from a shelf a huge jar of specimens in yellow alcohol.

"Take this fish," he said, "and look at it; we call it a haemulon; by and by I will ask what you have seen."

Observation #2

Figure 2-2. *Debbie Carpenter's Second Log (continued)*

With that he left me, but in a moment returned with explicit instructions as to the care of the object entrusted to me.

"No man is fit to be a naturalist," said he, "who does not know how to take care of specimens."

I was to keep the fish before me in a tin tray, and occasionally moisten the surface with alcohol from the jar, always taking care to replace the stopper tightly. Those were not the days of ground-glass stoppers and elegantly shaped exhibition jars; all the old students will recall the huge neckless glass bottles with their leaky, wax besmeared corks, half eaten by insects, and begrimed with cellar dust. Entomology was a cleaner science than ichthyology, but the example of the Professor, who had unhesitatingly plunged to the bottom of the jar to produce the fish, was infectious; and though this alcohol had a "very ancient and fishlike smell," I really dared not show any aversion within these sacred precincts, and treated the alcohol as though it were pure water. Still I was conscious of a passing feeling of disappointment, for gazing at a fish did not commend itself to an ardent entomologist. My friends at home, too, were annoyed when they discovered that no amount of eau-de-Cologne would drown the perfume which haunted me like a shadow.

In ten minutes I had seen all that could be seen in that fish, and started in search of the Professor—who had, however, left the Museum; and when I returned, after lingering over some of the odd animals stored in the upper apartment, my specimen was dry all over. I dashed the fluid over the fish as if to resuscitate the beast from a fainting fit, and looked with anxiety for a return of the normal sloppy appearance. This little excitement over, nothing was to be done but to return to a steadfast gaze at my mute companion. Half an hour passed—an hour—another hour; the fish began to look loathsome. I turned it over and around; looked it in the face— ghastly; from behind, beneath, above, sideways, at a three-quarters' view—just as ghastly. I was in despair; at an early hour I concluded that lunch was necessary; so, with infinite relief, the fish was carefully replaced in the jar, and for an hour I was free.

On my return, I learned that Professor Agassiz had been at the Museum, but had gone, and would not return for several hours. My fellow-students were too busy to be disturbed by continued conversation. Slowly I drew forth that hideous fish, and with a feeling of desperation again looked at it. I might not use a magnifying-glass; instruments of all kinds were interdicted. My two hands, my two eyes, and the fish: it seemed a most limited field. I pushed my finger down its throat to feel how sharp the teeth were. I began to count the scales in the different rows, until I was convinced that was nonsense. At last a happy thought struck me—I would draw the fish; and now with surprise I began to discover new features in the creature. Just then the Professor returned.

"That is right," said he; "a pencil is one of the best of eyes. I am glad to notice, too, that you keep your specimen wet, and your bottle corked."

With these encouraging words, he added:

"Well, what is it like?"

He listened attentively to my brief rehearsal of the structure of parts whose names were still unknown to me: the fringed gill-arches and moveable operculum; the pores of the head, fleshy lips and lidless eyes; the lateral line, the spinous fins and forked tail; the compressed and arched body. When I finished, he waited as if expecting more, and then, with an air of disappointment:

"You have not looked very carefully; why," he continued more earnestly, "you haven't even seen one of the most conspicuous features of the animal, which is plainly before your eyes as the fish itself; look again, look again!" and he left me to my misery.

I was piqued; I was mortified. Still more of that wretched fish! But now I set myself to my task with a will, and discovered one new thing after another, until I saw how just the Professor's criticism had been. The afternoon passed quickly; and when, toward its close, the Professor inquired:

"Do you see it yet?"

"No," I replied, "I am certain I do not, but I see how little I saw before."

"That is next best," said he, earnestly, "but I won't hear you now; put away your fish and go home; perhaps you will be ready with a better answer in the morning. I will examine you before you look at the fish."

This was disconcerting. Not only must I think of my fish all night, studying, without the object before me, what this unknown but most visible feature might be; but also, without reviewing my discoveries, I must give an exact account of them the next day. I had a bad memory; so I walked home by Charles River in a distracted state, with my two perplexities.

The cordial greeting from the Professor the next morning was reassuring; here was a man who seemed to be quite as anxious as I that I should see for myself what he saw.

"Do you perhaps mean," I asked, "that the fish has symmetrical sides with aspired organs?"

His thoroughly pleased "of course! of course!" repaid the wakeful hours of the previous night. After he had discoursed most happily and enthusiastically—as he always did—upon the importance of this point, I ventured to ask what I should do next.

"Oh, look at your fish!" he said, and left me again to my own devices. In a little more than an hour he returned, and heard my new catalogue.

"That is good, that is good!" he repeated; "but that is not all; go on"; and so for three long days he placed that fish before my eyes, forbidding me to look at anything else, or to use any artificial aid. "Look, look, look," was his repeated injunction.

This was the best entomological lesson I ever had—a lesson whose influence has extended to the details of every subsequent study; a legacy the Professor had left to me, as he has left it to so many others, of inestimable value, which we could not buy, with which we cannot part.

A year afterward, some of us were amusing ourselves with chalking outlandish beasts on the Museum blackboard. We drew prancing starfishes; frogs in mortal combat; hydra-headed worms; stately crawfishes, standing on their tails, bearing aloft umbrellas; and grotesque fishes with gaping mouths and staring eyes. The Professor came in shortly after, and was as amused as any at our experiments. He looked at the fishes.

"Haemulons, every one of them," he said; "Mr. _____ drew them."

True; and to this day, if I attempt a fish, I can draw nothing but haemulons.

The fourth day, a second fish of the same group was placed beside the first, and I was bidden to point out the resemblances and differences between the two; another and another followed, until the entire family lay before me, and a whole legion of jars covered the table and surrounding shelves; the odor had become a pleasant perfume; and even now, the sight of an old, six-inch, worm-eaten cork brings fragrant memories.

The whole group of haemulons was thus brought in review; and, whether engaged upon the dissection of the internal organs, the preparation and examination of the bony framework, or the description of the various parts, Agassiz's training in the method of observing facts and their orderly arrangement was ever accompanied by the urgent exhortation not to be content with them.

"Facts are stupid things," he would say, "until brought into connection with some general law."

At the end of eight months, it was almost with reluctance that I left these friends and turned to insects; but what I had gained by this outside experience has been of greater value than years of later investigation in my favorite groups.

*Lo*g Entry 5

There's certainly something positive to be said for Agassiz's method of teaching Scudder to become an attentive observer, but there might be some criticism, too. Take a few minutes and write your response to his method in your log. Since you have now had some experience in drawing your own subject, include comments on Agassiz's line, "A pencil is one of the best of eyes." Remember that in your log you are recording your own ideas and feelings. Ask yourself whether you think you would be patient enough to follow Agassiz's requests; or, if you did, would the results be worth it?

Remembered Observation: Memory of a Childhood Experience

One of the aspects of knowing that is completely omitted from Agassiz's method of observing the dead fish is observing the fish alive. Patrick Mebine knows the tiger swallowtail, a butterfly, in a very different way from the way Scudder knows his preserved dead fish. Mebine wrote this poem when he was a senior in high school. The assignment was, first, to recall a close observation of some kind of animal, then to sketch the animal as remembered, and finally to write about it in such a way as to reveal its impact on the observer. Here is his poem.

Tiger Swallowtail

Patrick Mebine

It rested upon an insignificant flower,
Only its wings visible,
Floating with the wind as if in flight,
Slicing the air with its brilliant
Yellow and blackest black stripes,
Enveloping my thoughts, leaving no others.

Not wanting it to leave my view,
Eyes transfixed, hands positioned, I moved.
Cupped hands felt fluttering beauty
large as themselves.

Beating its wings against the sides
Of the captive jar,
The tiger swallowtail constantly attempted escape.
The tiny feet could not cling to glass sides,
Its wings too large to open; even if they could,

Obstruction lay ahead, refusing passage
To air on which they floated,
Air whose rhythm the wings longed to
Beat against.

Now I wait for the moment:
Will my hands form wings?
Can the lid open the passage to freedom
As it did for the tiger swallowtail
So long ago?

I stare at you, transfixed;
I want to touch your beauty,
But I can only see you
Through the glass walls.

When is a poem a fish or a butterfly? The question of how we know an animal or an object is very much in the forefront of debates among scientists, philosophers, and literary critics. Some critics, for example, think of a poem as one of Agassiz's dead fish; others see the meaning of a poem only by looking at it in relation to the poet and the poet's life, as well as in relation to the reader and the reader's experience.

Collaborating

Use the discussion questions that follow as starters for thinking about how you can know something.

- Can we really know an animal apart from its environment?

- Can we know it apart from its behavior?

- Can we know it apart from our own reactions?

- What are your ideas about close observation in the laboratory as opposed to in the field?

- What do you think Scudder's reaction would be to Mebine's behavior? To his poem? We can't know, obviously, but we can learn something about both Scudder and Mebine by their writing. Which one would you rather talk with? Why?

• What do you think Patrick Mebine did with the swallowtail after he had captured it in a jar? What in the poem makes you think as you do?

*W*ork in Progress

Write a draft of a poem describing the subject you've chosen, as you know it so far. Use Mebine's poem as a model for observation, but not for story line. Try to describe the intricacies of what you have observed and your reaction to your observation. Put this work in your writing folder for later consideration

Secondhand Information: The Library

Now that you have observed your subject on two separate occasions and have thought a good deal about how we see and how we know, you have a good working knowledge of your subject—enough to know that there is more to know about it than you can see from external observations. For additional details, you need to consult information that other people have obtained through extended observations or through laboratory analysis.

*L*og Entry 6

Secondhand Information: Library Research

Using whatever resources your library offers, look up information about your subject. You may need help from the librarian in identifying the specific kind of animal or variety of plant you have been observing. There are books, for example, that let you look up a flower by its color, a tree by the shape of its leaves. Using your dual-entry notebook, record any data that adds to your own observations. The only criterion for your selection of data to record is whether you find it helpful in understanding your subject. For each resource you use (encyclopedia, field guide, essay, magazine) include the bibliographic data: title, author, publisher, date of publication, and page references.

Research Notes

Name of Subject of Research: _____ Date: _____	
Informative data Include specific information about your subject, along with reference data: title, author, publisher, date of publication, and page references.	*Personal response to data* Here you might record why a particular piece of information interested or surprised you. Should you find that the reference information disagrees with your own observations (and that may well happen), be sure to mention it.

Keep all of your research notes in your writing folder along with your personal observation logs. Figure 2-3 provides an example of one such log entry.

Firsthand Research: Back in the Field

*L*og Entry 7

Observation 3: Firsthand Information (continued)

Follow the same procedure as for your first two observations. In your double-entry notebook, you might note anything that you see differently now that you have read *about* your subject. Figure 2-4 shows how Debbie Carpenter continued.

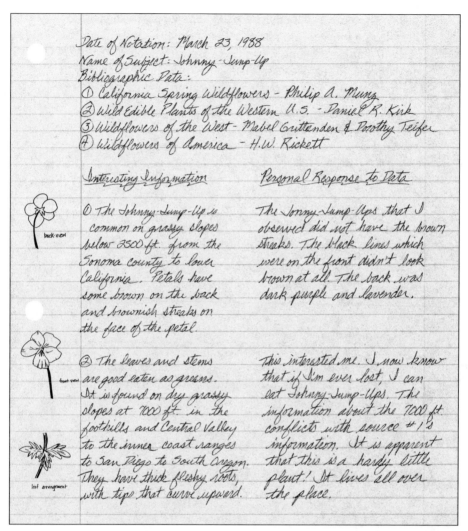

Date of Notation: March 23, 1988
Name of Subject: Johnny-Jump-Up
Bibliographic Data:
① California Spring Wildflowers - Philip A. Munz
② Wild Edible Plants of the Western U.S. - Daniel R. Kirk
③ Wildflowers of the West - Mabel Crittenden & Dorothy Teifer
④ Wildflowers of America - H.W. Rickett

Interesting Information

Personal Response to Data

① The Johnny-Jump-Up is
common on grassy slopes
below 3500 ft. from the
Sonoma county to lower
California. Petals have
some brown on the back
and brownish streaks on
the face of the petal.

The Johnny-Jump-Ups that I
observed did not have the brown
streaks. The black lines which
were on the front didn't look
brown at all. The back was
dark purple and lavender.

② The leaves and stems
are good eaten as greens.
It is found on dry grassy
slopes at 7000 ft. in the
foothills and Central Valley
to the inner coast ranges
to San Diego to South Oregon.
They have thick fleshy roots,
with tips that curve upward.

This interested me. I now know
that if I'm ever lost, I can
eat Johnny-Jump-Ups. The
information about the 7000 ft.
conflicts with source #1's
information. It is apparent
that this is a hardy little
plant! It lives all over
the place.

back view

front view

leaf arrangement

Figure 2-3. *Debbie Carpenter's Third Log*

Secondhand Information: Other People

We learn about something from our own observations, from reading
and library research, and also from talking with other people. Discuss the subject of your observations with at least two other people.
As you talk with them, explore whatever knowledge, personal mem-

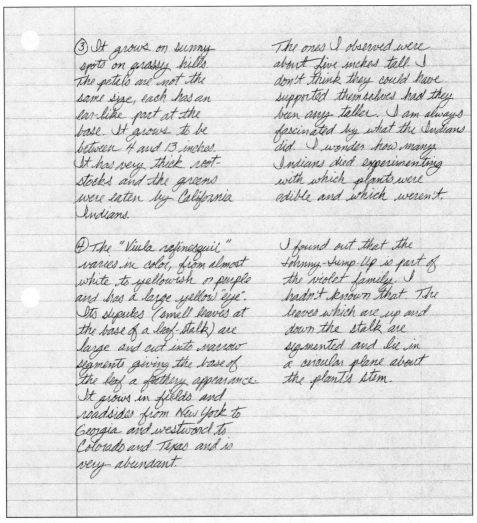

③ It grows on sunny spots on grassy hills. The petals are not the same size, each has an ear-like part at the base. It grows to be between 4 and 13 inches. It has very thick rootstocks and the greens were eaten by California Indians.

The ones I observed were about five inches tall. I don't think they could have supported themselves had they been any taller. I am always fascinated by what the Indians did. I wonder how many Indians died experimenting with which plants were edible and which weren't.

④ The "Viola rafinesquii" varies in color, from almost white to yellowish or purple and has a large yellow "eye". Its stipules (small leaves at the base of a leaf-stalk) are large and cut into narrow segments giving the base of the leaf a feathery appearance. It grows in fields and roadsides from New York to Georgia and westward to Colorado and Texas and is very abundant.

I found out that the Johnny-Jump-Up is part of the violet family. I hadn't known that. The leaves which are up and down the stalk are segmented and lie in a circular plane about the plant's stem.

Figure 2-3. *Debbie Carpenter's Third Log (continued)*

ories, and associations they are willing to share with you about your subject.

To prepare for your interview, work with a partner or small group to talk about some of the ways you can encourage people to talk to you about your subject. It would be helpful to check with the whole class to find out if anyone knows of a particular person who might

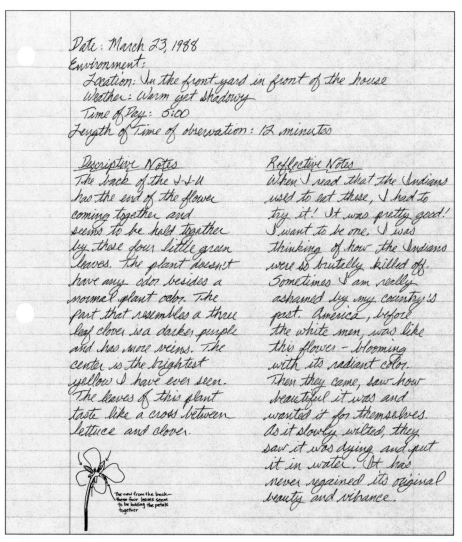

Figure 2-4. *Debbie Carpenter's Fourth Log*

be good to interview. Remember that this interview is a very informal discussion, not necessarily with an expert, but with someone who has had some experience observing your subject. In the case of a backyard tree, for example, you might find a neighbor who knows how it came to be planted where it was. If you are observing spi-

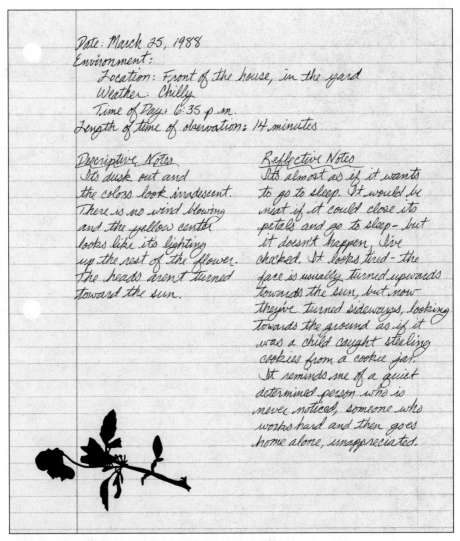

Date: March 25, 1988
Environment:
  Location: Front of the house, in the yard
  Weather: Chilly
  Time of Day: 6:35 p.m.
Length of time of observation: 14 minutes

Descriptive Notes
It's dusk out and the colors look irradescent. There is no wind blowing and the yellow center looks like it's lighting up the rest of the flower. The heads aren't turned toward the sun.

Reflective Notes
It's almost as if it wants to go to sleep. It would be neat if it could close its petals and go to sleep - but it doesn't happen, I've checked. It looks tired - the face is usually turned upwards towards the sun, but now they've turned sideways, looking towards the ground as if it was a child caught stealing cookies from a cookie jar. It reminds me of a quiet determined person who is never noticed, someone who works hard and then goes home alone, unappreciated.

Figure 2-4. *Debbie Carpenter's Fourth Log (continued)*

ders, you might ask a child to tell you about *Charlotte's Web*. You are looking for personal responses as well as any additional information about the history or habits of your subject.

Record your brief interviews in your double-entry log as follows:

Log Entry 8

Personal Interview Notes

Name of Subject of Research: _____

Date: _____

Person Interviewed: Brief notes about the person: for example, brother (age 11) or friend of my mother	*Ideas Contributed*: What did this person add to your knowledge or understanding of your subject? What associations or personal stories did this person tell you?

Add Log Entry 8 to your writing folder. Figure 2-5 is an example of this exercise.

Making Comparisons

One of the ways we learn to know a thing is to make comparisons between the object we are studying and something we already know about. Simple comparisons, *similes,* are so common in our everyday speech that we seldom stop to realize that we are actually comparing two things, or comparing some quality of one thing with the same quality of another. Similes usually operate on a descriptive level, comparing how one animal or object looks like or behaves like another. A negative simile points out qualities that distinguish something by separating it from something else that may share certain features.

Working either alone or with a partner, brainstorm as many possibilities for similes as you can for your object of study. Ask yourself, "What is it like?" "What is it unlike?" For example, a butterfly could be described as *like a dream* that is gone upon awakening, or *unlike butter,* which gave it its name in all ways except color.

Log entry #5	
Person Interviewed	Ideas Contributed
Mary Ellen Scott – teacher at Chipman Alias: "Mom"	Desc: Member of the violet family that is purple and yellow, or all yellow or violet and purple. There are many different violets-colors. It has a lot of blooms and if you pick off the dead ones, new ones will replace them. It has a short stem about 3 inches long. Thoughts: The name is very appropriate – it looks as if they're jumping up at you, even though it grows close to the ground. It is fragile looking but in reality is very healthy. All of the little faces are turned towards the sun. Memories: When she was in her flower pressing stage, these pressed the best because they retained their original color. She also remembers that her mother was the first one to tell her what they were called and bought her her first ones.

Figure 2-5. *Debbie Carpenter's Fifth Log*

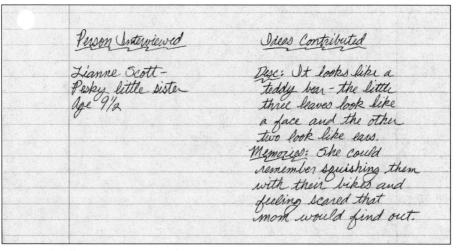

Figure 2-5. *Debbie Carpenter's Fifth Log (continued)*

*Lo*g Entry 9

Extending Comparisons

1. Select several of your similes, the ones you think are most
   promising for working into your writing, and record them in the
   left half of the chart that is Log Entry 9. Set it up as follows:

Name of Subject of Research: ＿＿＿＿＿＿＿＿	
Date: ＿＿＿＿＿＿＿	
Similes	*Metaphors*
Explanations	*Extensions of Metaphoric Ideas*
What is your subject like?	Brainstorm ideas for metaphors.
Write as many similes as you can.	Select the most promising
Explain your ideas about the most	metaphor.
promising similes.	
Follow your ideas as far as they	
will go.	

2. Now move from the small comparisons, the similes, to the more
   extended comparisons or *metaphors*. In a metaphor, the compari-
   son is implied; there is no expressed *like* or *as*. Although

metaphors are like similes in that they are comparisons based on some similarity between two things, a metaphor issues from more complex interactions of perceptions, feelings, and thoughts than is true for most similes. A good metaphor makes us think about our subject in a new way and often stimulates reflection. Although some metaphors, like the "flowering" of a life, may have been used a great deal in poetry, writers can often think of new ways to present metaphors. While one person might focus on the dropping of petals as a metaphor for death, another might focus on the petal dropping as the beginning of seed formation and the birth of a new life.

Think of possible metaphors for your subject, based on your experience of observing and researching your subject. Brainstorm possibilities with a partner. When you have generated a few possibilities, look at your list and decide which single metaphor seems to have the most potential for developing an observational poem or essay about your subject. Add your metaphor possibilities to the right half of the chart for Log Entry 9.

*G*raphic

Like the professionals, you now have a great deal more information about your animal, plant, or object than you will ever use in one piece of writing. To get a picture of what you know about your subject, make a *graphic map,* organizing the information from your log entries in a meaningful way. Use your most promising extended metaphor to help you formulate a focus for your map. For one student, the study of spiders suggested the focus of a web, with observations and research data written on the lines that formed the strands of the web. Observations of a vine, for another, contained several strands, one for personal observations, one for secondhand research, one for personal associations, and one for metaphorical comparisons—all written on hanging vine leaves. Let your imagination come up with interesting ways to organize the different aspects of your knowledge. Record only what you, in retrospect, find useful as you think about connecting your observations to your chosen metaphor.

Include one or more drawings of your subject and distinguish among the various ways of knowing—firsthand information, secondhand information, metaphor, personal associations, and memories. Include information about the environment, the effect of weather or light. Mapmaking is a process of synthesizing and selecting; include only information that you find helpful in knowing your subject, and present it as clearly as possible, differentiating the various kinds of information by design, color coding, or placement. If two or three of you in the class have studied the same subject, you might want to get together and draw a group map. Figure 2-6 provides an example.

Reflecting on Field Notes

Before you write your own essay or poem, you're going to look carefully at how one writer's personal observations and secondhand knowledge led, through an extended metaphor, to reflections about life in general. Read the following short essay from the column "Talk of the Town" in *The New Yorker* (September 4, 1971). Analyzing and modeling how one writer integrated personal observations with secondhand research and metaphorical ideas will give you inside information about one writer's thought progressions.

Field Notes on a Hummingbird

These field notes have come in from a bird-watcher on Martha's Vineyard: "The hummingbird builds her nest of cinnamon ferns and spider webs, shingled with lichens to resemble a small gnarl on a pine branch. Miraculously, we've spotted one just at eye level beside the dirt road that leads to the place we've rented here. Two white eggs, smaller than lima beans, have hatched, and the mother is whirring here and there faster than ever. (What a metabolism in those intense, short-lived, beautiful little beings!) For nectar, she has jewelweed, trumpet vine, and loose-strife flowering in the area; I have been told that she provides a slurry of bugs for her young. Mostly beak at this stage, they wait for her, motionless in the nest. And yet they'll be flying themselves within a week, and the migration schedule is such that they won't be found at all by mid-September. Of course, we won't be here to look for them. The summer always passes too rapidly, and I have been thinking that a *vacation,* with its concentration of compelling impressions, *can become a disquieting metaphor* for mortality itself. When it's

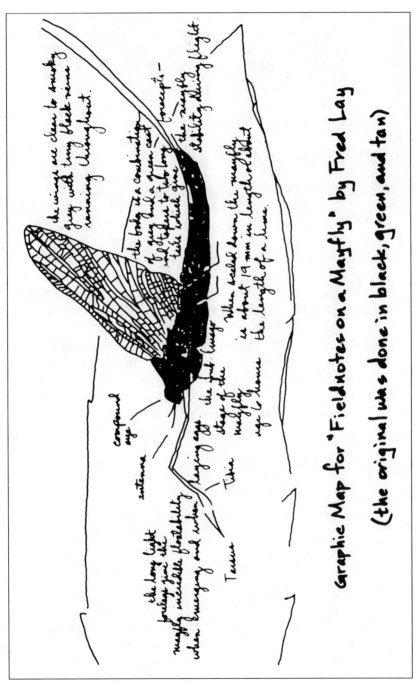

Figure 2-6. *Fred Lay's Graphic Map*

half gone, if the weather has been good and there have been no accidents, you think you'll still have ample time for everything you want to do. But then, suddenly, even though you haven't stopped enjoying yourself, you have to face the fact that in a limited number of days this period of freedom will be at an end. We've taken a picture of the hummingbird at work, but her wings beat maybe eighty times a second, and I had to warn the kids that even though we use the fastest shutter speed on our camera, there is sure to be a blur."

Analyzing Structure

Using your own field and research experience, work alone or with a partner to make detailed notes on how this writer's mind moved from one kind of knowing to another. In analyzing the thought progressions of "Field Notes on a Hummingbird," distinguish the different kinds of information each sentence or part of a sentence contains. Notice the firsthand or eyewitness observations about the ferns, spider webs, and lichens (lichens are a kind of fungus/alga combination, flat, like shingles) that the hummingbird uses to build her nest. You may have to make some guesses about whether information is first- or secondhand, but make your guesses logical. We know, for example, that the wildflowers *jewelweed, trumpet vine,* and *loose-strife* are growing in fields on Martha's Vineyard because the hummingbird drinks the nectar from them. It is logical, then, that the writer would have seen and identified these plants. Look for examples of all of the kinds of knowing you experienced in doing your field study:

- Firsthand information

- Secondhand information—research

- Secondhand information—other people

- Comparisons

- Metaphorical leaps through personal reflection or association

- Development of metaphor

If you have a photocopy of the essay, you can make your notes right on the essay itself. If you are working from the essay in the book, set up your analysis by jotting down the first words of a sentence on the left side of your paper and your identification of what kind of knowing led to the statement on the right. A couple of lines might look like this:

"The hummingbird builds her
nest of cinnamon ferns. . . ."   *Firsthand information*

"shingled with lichens to
resemble a small gnarl. . ."   *Simile*

Work through the entire essay this way, section by section, charting the structural sequence of the writer's thoughts.

Modeling the Essay

Modeling is one way of reading an essay from the inside out, from the author's perspective. Use the structural sequence you worked out for "Field Notes on a Hummingbird" as a rough guide for an essay about the plant, animal, or object that you have observed, studied, and mapped to include in your writing folder. Remember that you will use only a fraction of what you know about your subject. Your focus is to write an essay in which you use very close observations and other ways of knowing your subject (books, people, comparisons) to reflect on some aspect of your experience. Let your favorite metaphor be the springboard from observation to reflection. Suggested steps for writing your essay follow.

1. Chart the sections of your essay
List the kinds of information or thinking the author drew on as each appears sequentially in the hummingbird essay. Beside each notation, make notes, using your graphic map, of similar kinds of information that you might use in your essay. Notice how much of the essay is an expansion of the metaphor on the ephemeral quality of the hummingbird with, first, a vacation, then, more profoundly, the transitory aspects of human life.

2. Write a first draft
When you have blocked out the sequence of ideas, write a first draft out of your own field notes. Begin with "These field notes have come in from a . . ." Finish with a description of yourself as the naturalist and the location where you made your observations.

3. Try out your essay on a reader
Exchange first drafts with one or more members of your writing response group. Help each other revise the first draft by looking closely at revisions suggested by the following guidelines:

- Block out the structure of the paper and see how it moves through the stages of the model: opening, personal observation (interrupted by an exclamation as in the original essay), second-hand information, turning point, metaphor, expanded metaphor, personal observation.

- Identify the turning point, the sentence that moves from personal observation to reflection. If it is difficult to find, you might ask the writer to identify it for you.

- Look carefully at the last sentence: Is it a personal observation? In the original the last sentence depends for its meaning on the reader's understanding of the metaphorical subject of the essay. Does this sentence carry that implicit meaning? If not, you might have some suggestions to help the writer select a single observational detail that will carry the weight of the metaphor.

A student who completed this assignment has a message for you: "The hardest part for me, when I did this, was the last line. I got the idea that the last line was really important. It seemed simple at first because it was just another firsthand observation, but when we talked about it in groups, we realized that the wings beating too fast for the camera stood for the whole metaphor of life, of how it goes by too fast for us to get a picture of it. I had trouble doing that with my essay, but my partner and I worked on it and I think I got it."

Another student said, "Tell them not to forget the quotation mark at the end."

Had you noticed that the entire essay is in quotation marks, as if it were a letter that the writer is enclosing for us?

4. Revising for publication

After discussing your trial run with a partner or writing group, revise your essay until you are satisfied with it. Your teacher may decide to have the essays attached to the graphic maps on the bulletin board or to collect the essays in a class booklet. Following are two student examples of essays written as models of the hummingbird essay. The first one is by Debbie Carpenter, who contributed the log entries you have already seen. The second one is by Michael Hendron, who wrote this version for a state writing assessment after he had completed the field notes assignment in his class.

Field Notes on the Johnny-Jump-Up

Debbie Carpenter

These field notes have come in from a meadow hopper of Alameda's famous front yards: "The Johnny-jump-up is a small five petaled purple flower whose three main petals resemble the lucky Irish's four leaf clover. Incredibly, we've spotted a bright patch of them, which, if I remember correctly was there last year. Two small petals, smaller than sunflower seeds, peek out shyly between the main group of petals and the plant's small leaves blow softly in the ever-shifting breeze. (What endurance can be seen in those awe-inspiring little flowers!) Colorwise, the petals are a rich deep purple and the bright yellow center radiates its color onto the other petals making it a mirage of violet, yellow, and black; I have been told that it flowers year after year. These perennials grow in large bunches and seem to support each other as they are so tightly packed together. Right now, these flowers are in full bloom, radiating their bright colors to people passing by. Later, as the winds blow and the rain pours, this hearty plant seems to vanish as it lacks the companionship of warm weather and fresh spring breezes. It occurs to me that the spurts of growth and individuality of these plants interacting within the network of flowers can be seen as a metaphor for man's intellectual growth as well as his ability to coexist as an individual and a contributing member of society. When a person is a member of a group, he can expand and experience new things, but only up to a certain point. When this point is reached, the individual needs to step back from the group and reflect on himself and what he has learned. Only after this period of reflection can one go back to the group, contribute to it, and flourish once again. The group lends the individual strength and support in its fight to stand up for its own identity and beliefs. As I look upon the swaying bright mass of purple, an ever-shifting tide is created—one which sways dangerously close to the ground, only to be lifted up once again by the revitalizing breezes and the continual support of the tightly packed network of Johnny-jump-ups.

Field Notes on the Turkey Vulture
Observed on Las Trampas Ridge

Michael Hendron

My trek into the hills above my small town, away from all the traffic, has been worthwhile. I have just spotted two turkey vultures feeding on a dead animal, although they are too far away for me to see what animal it once was. The turkey vulture's scientific name is *cathartes aura* or "cleanser from the upper world," which seems most fitting since they eat the carrion which might otherwise decay and pose a health threat. They are not beautiful creatures, in fact, they are downright ugly with their naked, wrinkled heads, their hooked yellow beaks, their long, sharp talons and their dark feathers. But when these birds take wing and begin to fly, a transformation occurs. Like angels, they glide above the ground—so gracefully and peacefully. Two more vultures have just glided in from places unknown. They fly with their broad wings (their wingspan is almost six feet) held in a wide V position, floating effortlessly in rising currents of air, soaring in huge, endless circles. Above me they are scanning the ground below for any sign of death with their powerful black eyes, making invisible movements which somehow control their flight. Oh, how beautiful they are! I would give anything to be able to leap into the air and join them, but wouldn't we all? As I reflect upon this great desire—to fly on feathered wings like the turkey vultures—-I see it as a powerful metaphor for the great struggle of human existence itself: to be able to forget our own mundane state and be rid of our problems so that we might achieve something grand and glorious, almost spiritual. We build and fly planes and even hanggliders in an effort to break free from the ugliness of civilization, knowing that from above it takes on a new beauty. We try our best, but we are never able to reach that state of pure freedom the turkey vulture experiences. And in the end, we must always return to Earth. Our own grand desires are magnified a million times in the once-trivial lives of the turkey vultures. The sun is setting and I must leave now, but the vultures must also return home to their eggs, in some fall tree or beneath an overhanging cliff.

Seeing and Not Seeing

The eye is a complex organ, allowing images to travel to the brain in different ways. When we focus directly on something, we "see" primarily with the *cones,* cone-shaped cells in the retina that are sensitive to color and intensity. What we look at directly, we see in sharp outlines with clear delineations. When we are not focusing directly on something, however, the retina receives impressions through different cells, the *rods,* which are sensitive to low intensities of light. We see vague shapes, less distinct outlines, muted colors. Try the following experiment to get a sense of the difference between focused and unfocused seeing.

1. Sit up in your chair, with your feet on the floor, and relax your body, without slumping. Take two or three slow, deep breaths.

2. Select an object in the front of the room to focus on. You need to be able to see it clearly, without strain, and without moving your head.

3. Gaze steadily at this object without straining your eyes. Notice all of the details you can—lines, angles, curves, colors. You are now receiving clear images on the cones in your retina.

4. As your eyes begin to tire (the technical word is *fatigue*), let them droop slightly. (Don't go to sleep!) Let the object go slightly out of focus. You may find that you become more aware of the area around the object. During this kind of low-intensity vision, the rods in the retina are picking up the images.

5. Blink your eyes and focus again directly on the object. The environment may seem to disappear as the object clears.

Wallace Stevens calls this movement between focused and unfocused vision "a seeing and unseeing in the eye." While direct seeing—focusing on the size, shape, and color of an object or scene—lends itself to the kind of meticulous observations we have emphasized so far in this chapter, indirect "unseeing" can often reveal subtle qualities of feeling and tone. Stevens's poem "Thirteen Ways of Looking at a Blackbird" presents just such an example. Read this poem for tone and feeling—for the unseeing. Don't worry about understanding in the usual way.

Thirteen Ways of Looking at a Blackbird

Wallace Stevens

I
Among twenty snowy mountains,
The only moving thing
Was the eye of the blackbird.

II

I was of three minds,
Like a tree
In which there are three blackbirds.

III

The blackbird whirled in the autumn winds.
It was a small part of the pantomime.

IV

A man and a woman
Are one.
A man and a woman and a blackbird
Are one.

V

I do not know which to prefer,
The beauty of inflections
Or the beauty of innuendoes,
The blackbird whistling
Or just after.

VI

Icicles filled the long window
With barbaric glass.
The shadow of the blackbird
Crossed it, to and fro.
The mood
Traced in the shadow
An indecipherable cause.

VII

O thin men of Haddam,
Why do you imagine golden birds?
Do you not see how the blackbird
Walks around the feet
Of the women about you?

VIII

I know noble accents
And lucid, inescapable rhythms;
But I know, too,
That the blackbird is involved
In what I know.

IX
When the blackbird flew out of sight,
It marked the edge
Of one of many circles.

X
At the sight of blackbirds
Flying in a green light,
Even the bawds of euphony
Would cry out sharply.

XI
He rode over Connecticut
In a glass coach.
Once, a fear pierced him,
In that he mistook
The shadow of his equipage
For blackbirds.

XII
The river is moving.
The blackbird must be flying.

XIII
It was evening all afternoon.
It was snowing
And it was going to snow.
The blackbird sat
In the cedar-limbs.

In this poem, Stevens, who can be the most careful of direct observers, practices the art of unseeing. The title, "Thirteen Ways of
Looking at a Blackbird," is deliberately misleading. Stevens looks
everywhere and defines the blackbird by "unfocusing" until he has
thirteen different ways of looking and seeing. By focusing on the
background, a sense of the person's view of blackbirds emerges.

Work in Progress

To practice "unseeing," draft a parallel poem using the following
steps:

1. Select an object that you know well and try Stevens's technique of focusing on thirteen very specific ways of looking; each in some way will illuminate or define your subject.

2. Write up each of your thirteen "ways of looking" in short stanzas of one to three sentences each.

3. Try illustrating each stanza of your poem. You can either draw separate scenes or just use a few strokes of line and color to give quick impressions of each stanza. Some students have created mobiles of poems with each stanza hanging on a separate string, while others feel that pen and ink or watercolors best convey the impressionistic sense of their poems.

Here are two students' versions of thirteen ways of looking. In the first poem Scott Harper closely models Stevens's "Thirteen Ways of Looking at a Blackbird." In the second, Rebecca Hopkinson makes up an elaborate form, alternating single lines with a very specific stanza pattern using both rhythm and rhyme. Following her poem is her explanation of process, detailing how she went about composing it.

Mirror

Scott Harper

I look into the mirror
and see a face like my own.
Which is the reflection?

A reflection in the mirror.
It is not her own.
"Who's following me?!"

The deceased's room.
A mirror covered with powder.
Why do people hurt themselves?

In darkness,
does the mirror duplicate me?
If my back is turned,
does it contain my shadow?

Self-consciousness comes
from peers, and oneself.
When looking into a mirror,
one sees inadequacy.
In isolation, if a mirror is found,
does the owner feel
the same deficiency?

The clerk watches the boy
From the idle mirror.
How can a child live
in a world with no trust?

Broken mirror on the floor.
Shattered fragments of my fortune.

The circus mirror
reflects an unrecognizable image.
Through a small imperfection,
everything changes.
A twisted reality of life.

The water reflects.
Liquid glass.
Ripples destroy an image
never seen again.

Mirror.
Spegel.
Espejo.
Miroir.
Spiegel.
Falamin.
Mirror.

Helpless. Closing in. Afraid.
The mirror reflects light in my eyes.
Needles, scalpel, mirror.
Dentist devices of torture.

On the other side of the mirror,
is there another world copying our own?
Or are we the ones copying it?

Mirror:
The magic glass of a blind man's dream.

Theatre in Thirteen Eyes

Rebecca Hopkinson

I. The house that lived a thousand years, falls in a wave of ocean tears
And as we watch in anxious fear, the actor's voice makes waters rise
    And break and flood before our eyes.

II. Just as Nature envelopes all else, the stage is swallowed by voracious Nature.

III. The writer keeps a lively pen to keep our minds from out the fen
Giving birth and killing men, as actors suffer o'er their parts
    To press them further 'pon our hearts.

IV. A meal combines the goods of the earth; the theatre: those of the world.

V. Their bodies armed with weaponry, their minds awhirl with strategy,
The soldiers charge the enemy. Directors form a cunning plan
    To scourge the stage and spare no man.

VI. If the dark of night is coarse unsurety and the morning light a promise of quiet strength,
    Theatre is both sunrise and set.

VII. To turn base metals into gold to satisfy the kingly mold
Was noble game in days of old. Actors breathe life into the air,
    Make gold when dust is all is there.

VIII. The chill waters of the lake reflect what is best left untold; the theatre reflects everything.

IX. The ballerina concentrates, the breathless audience awaits
She leaps and soars, her fear abates. The actor pauses, flushing he,
    And leaps into soliloquy.

X. The empty man stands alone, the lone stage stands empty

XI. Four times a year the seasons change and with them moods do rearrange
Our feelings play a varied range. The actor turns from sun to rain
    To snow and air and back again.

XII. Do you watch theatre, or does the theatre watch you?

XIII. You've rowed to the end of the stream; you're nothing but wet, it would seem.
Life, they still say, is but a dream! As Robin makes his fond amends,
       Our simple play is at its end.

Why

Rebecca Hopkinson

On the very day we were given the assignment, I wrote a poem entitled "Thirteen Variations on Theatre," a very simple, dull work whose overall quality plainly revealed that its author was very simple and dull, or surprisingly complex and exciting and merely wearing the guise of a very simple, dull person. Two days after this was composed, it began to decompose and I was once again poemless. I remained in this state until Sunday, our final draft due the next day. My mother describes this as my "usual careful planning and foresight."

At 4:30 I sat down with a list of words. Theatre as: *music, dance, science, painting, writing, a game, war, life, weather, a natural disaster, a disease*. Looking away, I pointed at one of the words, which happened to be "natural disaster." I ransacked my mind for rhyme schemes and forms, and, not being able to twist my words around any of them, created the three-line, 50-syllable stanza, which may not really be my creation, but that's hardly the point.

I tentatively wrote the first line, dredged up two rhyming words and fumbled around with lines until I had something worthy of recording. For the next two and a half hours, and three and a half hours after my quesedilla[sic]/"60 Minutes" break, I continued to write in that form, some stanzas manifesting themselves on the paper before I had due time to think, others rolling around inside my head for half an hour before I got the first line straight. After seven of these stanzas and aches in the joints of my hand, I discovered that I was tired and in no state to spend another six hours writing, so I used my method of choosing topics from the list, wrote six sentences that sounded as though they might mean something, arranged the poem into its present order, copied it, and smiled myself to sleep.

Some of the choices I made in use of punctuation are credited to T. E. Lawrence, whose epic *Seven Pillars of Wisdom* introduced me to the beauty of the colon and semicolon, and was in turn introduced to them by George Bernard Shaw. Some of the words, "fen" being one

of them, rhymed with my first line, and I supposed that it was actually a word so I looked it up and found its meaning quite useful. The
rest is simply my vocabulary, knowledge, and use of words, none of
which, in my opinion, are entirely deserving of such praise as they
have just received. And this is not modesty: know that much.

Sometimes an image from our memory just presents itself as a
poem when we least expect it—while we are riding along the freeway or sitting at home reading the newspaper. The next poem happened that way. Peter Stillman read in the paper that scientists no
longer believe groups rely on leaders. In an article describing the
flocks and schools of thousands of birds and fish, the reporter wrote
that researchers are only beginning to understand the complexity
and synchronization that enables 10,000 starlings to wheel in formation over a cornfield. The images in the article triggered an
image in Peter's memory, resulting in this poem:

Outside a house
I lived in once
some starlings school across
a yellow sky

the whole of them
turning like
a single thought

a law come into being
the birds being words
in the law

It was probably a very similar sight that Joyce Spreyer recalled
when she wrote her poem "Blackbirds."

Blackbirds
Joyce Spreyer

A wheel of blackbirds
turns
slicing sky.

The formation
dissolves:
birds light
on the naked crossbeams
of a half-built house.

I stop—
remembering
this place: the old oak,
branches black with birds;
fragile
dun-colored nests that clung
to clumps of grass, riding
the wind.

Once I watched a single bird,
wings aflame,
drive the others, one by one,
out of the oak
beyond invisible fences
strung with song.

The oak is gone now,
the earth scraped
clean. Skeleton limbs
are black with birds.

Peter Stillman's starlings turned like "a single thought," while
Joyce Spreyer's "wheel of blackbirds / turns / slicing sky." John Up-
dike referred to such a mass of birds forming a single thought as "a
scarf of birds." The next time you see a great multitude of birds,
look and ask yourself the question the scientists ask: What impulse
drives these birds to act in unison? It may be that the scientist/poet
who sees them as some variation of "a scarf," "a single thought," or
"a wheel" will write another poem about blackbirds. The same sci-
entist/poet may well come upon the metaphor that leads to scientific understanding of this as yet mysterious phenomenon.

Log Entry 10

For the next few days, keep your log handy as you walk or ride to
school, read your history or science homework, watch television, or
read the paper. Notice when something you see or read triggers an
image from your memory—something you probably have never focused on but carried around with you buried somewhere among the
billions of neurons in your brain. Jot the image down. Then, when

you have time, try extending the image, as Peter Stillman did with
the image of the school of starlings, letting it turn into a thought, a
"law" formed of birds/words.

Building Your Course Portfolio

As the last project of this chapter, you will add to your portfolio the
finished field notes essay and a selection of other writing that grew
out of your observations and reflections. It should represent your
best work and become an evaluation of your work over the course
of this chapter. You may want to review the introduction to the
course portfolio in the first chapter of this book.

Revising and Editing

Using your log and works in progress from your writing folder, look
at all the possibilities you have generated during your work in this
chapter. Some pieces may well be finished already; other promising
pieces may at present be notations in your log. Since the portfolio
represents your best work, the writing you want to share with others, your goal now is to select those pieces that you want to work
on. You may want to include some of your log entries as well as the
poems, memory writings, stories, or essays that you began. Get together with the other members of your writing group so that you
can help evaluate each other's work. Preparing the portfolio may involve some extended revising and editing; in this process, use the
help of your writing group.

Reflecting

Create a new section in your portfolio labeled Chapter 2. Then,
when you've made all of your selections—reading, writing, and
graphic—arrange the pieces in an order that suits you and prepare
a table of contents. Write an introductory essay reflecting on what
you've chosen to place in the portfolio and why. This essay should
convey to the readers of your portfolio—other members of your
class, your teacher, perhaps friends and members of your family—
your best thinking and writing. Since this chapter was concerned
with helping you develop your powers of vision, we hope that the
portfolio will reveal your sensitivity and skills as a careful observer.

3

Landscape and Identity

*S*o far in this book, you have focused on your perceptions of nature and your reflections about the world around you. Now we're going to ask you to shift your lens slightly, to focus instead on yourself in relationship to the world around you. Of course, your perceptions come from who you are, so you certainly haven't been observing and reflecting without realizing that who you are shapes what you see. We want you to think about the relationship between the landscapes around you and your identity.

Exactly what do we mean by *landscapes*? Defined broadly, we mean your surroundings—geographical, historical, and interpersonal. How have the places where you have lived helped shape who you are? What influences come from the past? From other people?

Who we are is often defined by where we're from—at least by others. In *Blue Highways: A Journey into America*, William Least Heat Moon talks about such geographical perceptions. He has stopped in Tennessee at a roadside cafe for breakfast where the waitress asks him if he's from the North. He replies, "I guess I am," and tells the reader, "A Missourian gets used to Southerners thinking him a Yankee, a Northerner considering him a cracker, a Westerner sneering at his effete Easternness, and the Easterner taking him for a cowhand." (The entire excerpt appears in the next chapter of this text.)

What qualities are associated with each of these stereotypes? What does it mean to be a "Yankee" or a "cowhand"? What geographical stereotypes do you know of? Take a few minutes to discuss this with the rest of the class. Then think about and discuss whether all characteristics must be stereotypes. For example, are there certain qualities that can reasonably be associated with people from certain parts of this country or from other parts of the world? How might the geography have demanded particular qualities from those who needed to survive there? Do you have particular characteristics or values that you can trace to geographical influences?

In this chapter, we'll explore the relationships between landscapes and identity through reading various texts that require you to use your imagination. And we'll ask you to approach your reading through an angle you may not have tried much—performance. If "performance" conjures up visions of producing full-length plays, memorizing lengthy speeches, wearing makeup, and standing under hot lights in front of hundreds of people, you're not perceiving it the same as we are. For the purposes of this chapter, we are talking merely about using your voice and your body to respond to and interpret the literature that you read.

Seeing and Performing

You may have been introduced at an early age to the dramatic power of the human voice. Many of us remember the pleasure of a trusted adult—mother, father, teacher—reading aloud to us. *Where the Wild Things Are* may have come to life first through the voice of another reader. The rhythm and rhyme of *The Cat in the Hat* are even more important than the words themselves. Perhaps we first heard folk tales in our ancestors' native languages, learning about humans interacting with coyotes, turtles, dragons, frogs, or cranes.

Although some might scoff that reading aloud is "kid stuff," many people attest to the popularity of listening to literature. Teens and adults purchase millions of dollars' worth of tape-recorded books each year. Driving or jogging, they listen to books and, possibly, remember the pleasure of the first time someone read aloud to them. They know that listening to literature read well is pleasurable for all ages.

In this chapter we hope you will find that reading aloud to interested listeners can be a performance as much as acting or singing might be. We hope that you will also discover that reading aloud is another way of interpreting literature—another angle of vision. The way you read the words demonstrates your understanding of the text. In addition, trying out different ways of reading a poem or story may help you arrive at additional understandings. Occasionally, it is helpful to get up and move around as you try to envision the exact positions of characters in relation to each other or as you try to imagine the effect an author wanted to create through the posture or gesture of a particular person or speaker.

If you think about it, it is nearly impossible simply to read a story in the sense that most of us understand the term "reading"—a set of word recognition skills and vocabulary useful in reading for information and correct answers. This is one kind of reading, but it is far different from what happens when we create new meanings of our own from a text—when a single line or even one word can stir in us eager leaps of the imagination beyond the specifics of the story or poem or play.

As we *react* we also *enact*. That is, when we read and react to what we've read, we stage performances in what is often called "the theater of the mind." The reading of fiction nearly always amounts to a performance in this imagined theater—where we see and hear not only what the author may have perceived in his or her imagination, but also (or even instead) what we bring to the reading from our own backgrounds.

Landscapes of Memory

Our memories make up part of the background that we bring to observation and imagination. What we remember and the emotions associated with events and people from our past shape who we are now. Bill McBride demonstrates this interplay of past and present, memory and reality in "I Remember."

I Remember
Bill McBride

As I watch you now,
    not remembering where the silverware is kept
    or how the knives and forks are placed,
I remember when such a common task was pure reflex.

As I hear you now,
    asking which pan to use
    or how to peel the potatoes or turn the stove on,
I remember American enchiladas, homemade wedding cakes,
    and T-bone steaks for breakfast.

As I talk with you now,
    reminding you again and again
    who your visitors are and
    what your yesteryears involved,
I remember frosted cake pans, antique tan dresses,
    and postcard messages gone awry.

Now that you live in a fleeting, fragmented present tense,
I remember—for both of us.

Log Entry 1

1. Jot down your initial reaction to the poem.

2. Look over what you have written and focus on one word. Maybe it stands out because you can think of more you would like to say about it or it intrigues you because you wonder why you

wrote that particular word or maybe it's a word from the poem that you would like to explore further. Freewrite for five minutes about that word as a way of expanding your thinking about the poem. This is called a *focused freewrite*.

Collaborating

In small groups of three to five:

1. Discuss your reactions to the poem, including questions you have. You may or may not want to share the results of your focused freewrite.

2. Who do you think the speaker is? How old? What does the speaker look like? Think about how the speaker would say each of the lines and stanzas. Discuss the best way to express each line, given the identity that you believe the speaker has. For example, would your tone change within each stanza when the speaker says "I remember"? What feeling would you want to convey?

Work in Progress

What do *you* remember? What specific sights, sounds, smells, and tastes contribute to your memory? How does what you remember relate to who you are now? Draft your own "I Remember" poem, incorporating concrete details of one part of the landscape of your memory. Your poem can be as short as McBride's poem or as long as—or longer than—the two poems in the following section. Your purpose is to demonstrate a contrast between then and now, using vivid details that help the reader visualize the interplay between memory and identity. You may decide to read this poem aloud to your group or your class, refine the draft for your portfolio, or just leave it in your writing folder.

An Oral Collage

Occasionally, poems take on additional meanings when they are read together. First, read aloud each of the next two memory poems separately and then follow the directions on pages 82–83 for creating an oral collage.

A Life of Evolution
Charles Alexander

I remember a simpler time
When all that troubled my heart
Were the social graces of being six.

I remember a time before
I knew about sex, race or THE HATE
Of bigotry, homophobia, sexism or ignorance.

I remember a time of wonder,
Discovery, being carefree when
I ran on the playground basking in the sun.

I remember a time
When Blacks and Whites walked hand in hand
When the "Dream" was a reality for me.

Yes, I remember, but then . . .
CORRUPTION!
Racism crashed down.

I remember the first time
I became aware that I was Black
And hence . . . different.

I remember the lies in school,
"You came here on the Mayflower,
Europe is your heritage."

I remember asking
"Why are all the great men white,
Where are the ones who look like me?"

I remember that all-White school
Being called names: Nigger, rug-head, monkey man.
Humiliation was the rule.

I remember being told
"Go back to Africa you F——
Spear chucking jigaboo."

Yes, I remember, but then
DISCOVERY at age ten
When my father taught me about Africa.

I remember the African music,
Jazz, blues, R&B and rap
When the rhythm touched my soul.

I remember Black pride
Afros, dashikis—the discovery of
Mother Africa.

I remember Dr. King,
Malcolm X, my father,
My grandfather and his father.

I remember discovering my history.
I remember discovering my warrior within,
I remember overcoming ignorance and fear.

I Remember Junior High

Antonette Aragon

I remember the days I could not wait.
Wait for school to end.
School was boring,
Junior high that is.

I remember the crowded school
and the boring teachers
and my friends.
My friends were fun
but sometimes they were mean.
My friends laughed at me
because I had hairy legs
and I still liked my roller skates, dolls and bike.
My friends liked dates, trips to malls, and Mike Dike.

I remember wanting to be smart
but teachers told me I could not be on the fast track.
I did not care what they said
and I signed up anyway.
I am Mexican and I am smart.

The days were long and school was boring.
But Mrs. Garcia said school is short and so is life.
I remember junior high.
That's all that I remember.

Collaborating

- Discuss these two poems with a partner. How do you envision the speakers? Describe their physical characteristics, their ages, and their attitudes.

- How would you describe the tone of each poem? You can often discern different tones as a poem is read aloud—bitter, sarcastic, nostalgic, enthusiastic, and so on.

- Are there words or phrases that you are uncomfortable saying aloud? Why might the poets have included those words or phrases? What effect do they have on the rest of the poem?

Performance

Using these two poems, create an oral collage by having two speakers, possibly a male and a female, read alternate lines or stanzas. One pattern would be to have the first speaker read the first stanza of Aragon's poem, beginning "I remember the days I could not wait." The second reader would then read the first three stanzas of Alexander's poem. Then the first reader would continue with, "I remember the crowded school." The reading could continue alternating stanzas and speakers in this way to the end of the poem. Or, create your own variations, depending on the tones you identified and the effect you wish to create.

As a class, discuss the effect of the different readings. How did the meaning or mood of the poems change for each variation? Do you prefer one manner of presenting the poems? Why?

Portfolio Entry

If you want to explore this idea further, you might form a small group to create your own oral collage. Using your "I Remember" poems or other poems that you select or write, try different ways of combining the texts. When you have the combination that you prefer, record it and/or present it to the class. Your recording could go into your portfolio as a demonstration of what you know and are able to do with oral reading.

Many Voices, Many Meanings in Performance

In this part of the chapter, you will focus on the voices in literature. When you're only reading words on the page, you're missing an important dimension of interpretation—the voices behind the words. We each have a distinctive voice quality. From our voices, listeners estimate our geographical origin, age, social status, health, and even mood. Good oral readers train their voices to convey a range of these and other qualities. That doesn't mean you have to be an impersonator or mimic; it does mean that you should attempt to make your character's voice fit his or her personality in convincing ways.

Experienced readers know that the words on a page can reveal live characters speaking in many voices. Through reading, we begin to liberate those characters, to give them form and flesh and voice. We try to understand their personalities. And, when deciding to present those characters to an audience of one or more, we share our understanding and appreciation of the literature we perform.

In this section of the chapter, you will learn about one way to do that—Readers Theater. This is a special kind of reading-aloud performance sometimes called Theater of the Imagination or Theater of the Mind because it capitalizes on the imaginations of the audience. Costumes, props, and sets somewhat limit—even determine—our interpretation of traditional plays, but no such constraints apply to this type of performance. The actors sit on stools or stepladders or risers, reading from their scripts and providing characterization through facial expressions, voice, and body language rather than through costumes and movements.

Scripts differ as well. While plays can be used, so can all sorts of other literature—short stories, song lyrics, poems, letters, diaries, essays, and newspaper stories. A narrator can be added to provide transition between selections or details of setting or situation that the characters themselves can't convey. The variety of available script material makes Readers Theater a good vehicle for understanding all sorts of prose and poetry, not just plays. And, an added advantage is that scripts don't need to be memorized.

Another difference between traditional theater and Readers Theater is that the actor's voice, while always important, becomes even more so. Without props, makeup, or costumes, the voice becomes the primary means of bringing characters to life for the audience.

Even though you will be holding your script and won't need to memorize it, you will need to know it very well. After all, you are supposed to be the character, and few real, live people sound as though they're reading lines when they're talking.

Before putting together a full script, though, you may want to complete some preliminary activities.

Thinking About Performing

You might be uncomfortable about getting up in front of the class, especially if you think you'll be laughed at or graded. Neither should happen to you. If you're a little nervous, think about why you feel that way and what kind of performances you would be comfortable doing. Could you perform in a small group? As part of a larger group or the whole class? Maybe you're excited about performing. What can you do to make others as excited and comfortable as you are?

If you discuss some of these questions in a small group or as a whole class, you'll probably discover that you're not alone in your feelings. Everyone, even experienced performers, feels some stage fright before going in front of an audience or a camera. In fact, some nervousness is good because it causes your adrenaline to flow, giving your performance a little extra energy. With practice, most people learn to control their feelings enough that stage fright does not incapacitate them.

*Lo*g Entry 2

Besides the nervousness or excitement you might feel, there are other ways in which performing literature is different from reading it. Think of several ways in which this is true. Take a few minutes to list those ways in your log. Make a T-chart like the one below and list all the differences between reading and performing literature that you can think of. Then discuss your findings with others.

Reading	*Performing*

Voice Exercises

The activities in this chapter will not train you as an actor, but they are meant to help you enjoy and understand literature through the dimension of performance. Thus it is helpful to do some of the voice exercises that trained performers use.

*Co*llaborating

With your partner or in a small group:

1. Imagine the personality behind each of the following phrases. You might be a spoiled child, an irritable businessman, or an energetic cheerleader. Any distinctive type that you imagine (without engaging in cruel stereotyping) will probably work.

- I'm tired.

- What do you mean?

- Who are you?

- I have something to tell you.

- Where are you going?

2. Say each phrase in two or three different ways.

3. Discuss the exercise after everyone has practiced. How does the meaning of the phrase change as you change characters? Although you say the same phrase each time, what is a businessman thinking when he says, "I'm tired"? What does a spoiled child mean by the same phrase? How can you use your voice to reveal the thoughts behind the words?

Your group may want to do additional voice exercises for practice. Any drama book will offer a wealth of choices. You might practice saying tongue twisters to improve your articulation (ability to say words clearly) or recite nursery rhymes, standing at some distance from your audience, to improve your ability to project your voice.

Producing a Readers Theater Program

In producing a Readers Theater program, you will use several tools to help you understand and enjoy what you read. There are some guidelines in this section for selecting material and converting it to a script. In the process of adapting material, you'll notice that thinking through and discussing literature improves your performance of it, and performing it increases your understanding. Besides, you may enjoy it.

Selecting material

Experience can guide you here. As a class, discuss considerations when selecting literature for an audience. What sorts of stories, poems, and plays are you interested in? Who will the audience be? What are they interested in? How would your material differ if you were preparing a program for a group of fourth graders rather than a group of high school students? What if your audience were all senior citizens? Or if the audience were all male or all female? Suppose that instead of performing for members of an English class, you were reading for a social studies class. Take the time to deal thoughtfully and specifically with these considerations.

*Lo*g Entry 3

Summarize the key aspects of the discussion. You might begin by completing these two sentence stems: "The audience partially determines the selection because . . ." and "Literature for performance should have these characteristics: . . ." Don't stop with those sentence stems, though, and don't even use them if they don't fit the discussion your class had. What is important here is the summary of your own discussion.

Adapting material

When you have selected your material, you need to adapt it for performance. You may choose one long selection or compile a script from many shorter selections. Whichever you do, there are additional choices to make:

- Decide how to break the selection into lines for characters if necessary. Some selections, such as plays, may already have lines divided for you.

- Decide where the climax or climaxes are in the piece; you'll need to build to them by raising your voice, adjusting your emphasis, or using some other means as you read.

- Decide how to handle action. A narrator might tell about it, or the actors might suggest it through various poses or a series of frozen pictures (tableaux) that change for each scene, or through minimal movements. Be creative; use your imagination to stimulate the audience's imagination.

The following scripts offer some ways to elicit voices from a poem that doesn't have any dialogue. As you try out the different scripts, consider how the surroundings define the people in the poem. What perspectives does the poem add to the theme of "learning the landscape"? (Script 1 follows the stanza breaks of the poem.)

Collaborating

With your partner or in a small group:

1. Read each script.

2. Discuss the questions that follow.

3. Write your conclusions in your log.

Script 1:

[*Reader 1:*]

Abandoned Farmhouse
Ted Kooser

He was a big man, says the size of his shoes
on a pile of broken dishes by the house;
a tall man too, says the length of the bed
in an upstairs room; and a good, God-fearing man,
says the Bible with a broken back
on the floor below the window, dusty with sun;
but not a man for farming, say the fields
cluttered with boulders and the leaky barn.

[*Reader 2:*]
A woman lived with him, says the bedroom wall
papered with lilacs and the kitchen shelves
covered with oilcloth, and they had a child
says the sandbox made from a tractor tire.
Money was scarce, say the jars of plum preserves
and canned tomatoes sealed in the cellar-hole,
and the winters cold, say the rags in the window frames.
It was lonely here, says the narrow gravel road.

[*Reader 3:*]
Something went wrong, says the empty house
in the weed-choked yard. Stones in the fields
say he was not a farmer; the still-sealed jars
in the cellar say she left in a nervous haste.
And the child? Its toys are strewn in the yard
like branches after a storm—a rubber cow,
a rusty tractor with a broken plow,
a doll in overalls. Something went wrong, they say.

*L*og Entry 4

What is the logic of this division? Discuss why it does or does not
strike you as providing appropriate dramatic effect to the piece.
Does it, as divided here, lend itself to performing?

Script 2:

[*Reader 1:*]

Abandoned Farmhouse
Ted Kooser

He was a big man, says the size of his shoes
on a pile of broken dishes by the house;
a tall man too, says the length of the bed
in an upstairs room; and a good, God-fearing man,
says the Bible with a broken back
on the floor below the window, dusty with sun;
but not a man for farming, say the fields
cluttered with boulders and the leaky barn.

[*Reader 2:*]
A woman lived with him, says the bedroom wall
papered with lilacs and the kitchen shelves
covered with oilcloth,

[*Reader 3:*]
and they had a child
says the sandbox made from a tractor tire.

[*Reader 2:*]
Money was scarce, say the jars of plum preserves
and canned tomatoes sealed in the cellar-hole,
and the winters cold, say the rags in the window frames.
It was lonely here, says the narrow gravel road.

[*Reader 1:*]
Something went wrong, says the empty house
in the weed-choked yard. Stones in the fields
say he was not a farmer;

[*Reader 2:*]
the still-sealed jars
in the cellar say she left in a nervous haste.

[*Reader 3:*]
And the child? Its toys are strewn in the yard
like branches after a storm—a rubber cow,
a rusty tractor with a broken plow,
a doll in overalls. Something went wrong, they say.

*Lo*g Entry 5

Does this version represent better or worse the logical breaks or shifts
in the poem? Does each reader have an equal share? Does it seem
more like a play or a reading? Are there advantages either dramatically or thematically to this division over the first one? For example,
do you know any more about the characters or why they left? Does
the characterization seem to be as distinct as in the first version?

Script 3:

[*Reader 1:*]

Abandoned Farmhouse
Ted Kooser

[*Reader 2:*]
He was a big man,

[*Reader 4:*]
(echoes) a big man

[*Reader 1:*]
says the size of his shoes
on a pile of broken dishes by the house;

[*Reader 2:*]
a tall man too,

[*Reader 4:*]
(echoes) a tall man

[*Reader 1:*]
says the length of the bed
in an upstairs room;

[*Reader 2:*]
and a good, God-fearing man,

[*Reader 3:*]
(echoes) good and God-fearing

[*Reader 1:*]
says the Bible with a broken back
on the floor below the window, dusty with sun;

[*Reader 2:*]
but not a man for farming,

[*Reader 1:*]
say the fields
cluttered with boulders and the leaky barn.

[*Reader 3:*]
A woman lived with him,

[*Reader 1:*]
says the bedroom wall
papered with lilacs and the kitchen shelves
covered with oilcloth,

[*Reader 4:*]
and they had a child

[*Reader 1:*]
says the sandbox made from a tractor tire.

[*Reader 3:*]
Money was scarce,

[*Reader 1:*]
say the jars of plum preserves
and canned tomatoes sealed in the cellar-hole,

[*Reader 2:*]
and the winters cold,

[*Readers 3 and 4:*]
oh, so cold

[*Reader 1:*]
say the rags in the window frames.

[*Reader 3:*]
It was lonely here,

[*Readers 3 and 4:*]
so lonely

[*Reader 1:*]
says the narrow gravel road.

[*All:*]
Something went wrong,

[*Reader 1:*]
says the empty house
in the weed-choked yard.

[*Reader 2:*]
Stones in the fields
say he was not a farmer;

[*Reader 3:*]
the still-sealed jars
in the cellar say she left in a nervous haste.

[*Reader 4:*]
And the child? Its toys are strewn in the yard
like branches after a storm—a rubber cow,
a rusty tractor with a broken plow,
a doll in overalls.

[*All:*]
Something went wrong, they say.

[*Reader 4:*]
(*echoes*) Something went wrong.

*L*og Entry 6

Are there advantages either dramatically or thematically to this division over the other two? For example, do you know any more about the characters or why they left? Do you know more about how the characters feel? Does characterization seem to be more distinct? Who do you think readers three and four are? How would you change the divisions if you believed the wife and child left because the man took out his frustrations on them?

Putting It All Together

Because the focus throughout the chapter has been on the relationship of imagination to performance and how developing that relationship can help you understand and enjoy literature, the suggestions that follow are designed for classroom performance. If you want to know more about full-scale Readers Theater productions, check your school's drama department or a school or public library. However, if you've done the exercises in this section and you use your creativity, you should have a program that will entertain and inform any audience that sees it. The following steps will help you prepare.

1. Form groups of three to five to prepare a performance

2. Select a script
You might find already-published scripts that you like. Or you may choose to write or compile a script of your own.

3. Analyze the script
Your knowledge of literature will help. You probably already know something about point of view, theme, tone, mood, and characteri-

zation as they apply to literary selections. Apply that knowledge to your Readers Theater script. Only if you know the selection thoroughly will you be able to convey its intricacies to the audience.

Here's a sample analysis for "Abandoned Farmhouse."

> *Point of view:* The speaker is an outside observer who knows no more than the reader. All of the speaker's information comes from an unknown "they" and the speaker's own observations.
>
> *Theme:* Possibly, how little outsiders know of the relationships within families, or the tragedy of the farm crisis that forces families to abandon their livelihood.
>
> *Tone:* Objective; it's a series of images pieced together for a total picture.
>
> *Mood:* Loneliness, sadness, uneasiness because of the mystery about what really happened.
>
> *Characterization:* A speaker and three characters—man, woman, and child. The child may be a girl because of the doll in overalls. The man seems to be a failure at what he does, but he is large and stern. The woman tries to decorate only the bedroom and the kitchen. Motivation must be inferred, but it is quite important. Why did the events in the poem happen? Why did the people do what we assume they did? There are broken dishes and a broken-backed Bible on the floor that indicate the man might have had a temper. That is supported by the woman's leaving in "nervous haste." Perhaps they did not all leave together.

Analyze each of these elements in the script you plan to use. Record your analysis in your notebook before you go on.

4. Stage the production

Earlier in the chapter you learned that Readers Theater productions generally use few props, costumes, or lights. The fact that you need only a few tools or chairs and perhaps some music stands for the scripts makes this kind of production possible for groups that may not have the budget, time, or desire to stage a full-scale production.

The absence of many traditional staging devices makes the suggestive use of a few elements more dramatic. If you have a stage bare of everything except the actors, they will obviously be more prominent. If you add a simple spotlight, you have increased the importance of whatever or whomever you choose to highlight. If you pantomime most props, the one prop you do have will appear to be important. For example, what prop might the child hold during the performance of "Abandoned Farmhouse"? Why would you select that one? What makes it more dramatic than another one or no prop at all?

You might also use music and sound effects dramatically. Each production will have specific characteristics determined by the director and the actors, so it's not possible to tell you what music to use or what sound effects you'll want to employ. Keep in mind that your primary goal is to help the audience imagine the world that the author created. Use whatever staging techniques or tools you think will help. But remember to use them as tools, not gimmicks. The audience should never be consciously aware of the elements of the performance; instead, they should be focused on the total performance.

A final, and the most important, element of staging is the actors. Where are they? What do they do? How do they "act"? Again, the best advice is the least advice. Experiment. Try several different approaches before deciding on one. Think about the effects of each approach. Should the actors be on different levels using stepladders or risers? Where should they focus? If the actors look at each other, the audience may feel it is watching someone perform for them. If the actors look directly at the audience, they may seem to be individuals rather than a group. If they look at points at particular spots in the auditorium, the audience may feel invited to imagine the same picture the actors are imagining. Depending on the situation and the purpose of the production, each of these focuses can be effective. How far apart will the actors be seated? Will you vary the distances to show relationships? How many readers do you need? Will some read more than one part?

This may seem like a dizzying array of decisions. But, when you begin producing a script, the decisions should fall into place. You need to know your options, but you also need to know that you have the power to be as creative as your imagination and resources allow. Try several approaches.

One final word to the actors. Remember that you are doing far more than reading aloud. You want to recreate the author's meaning and your interpretation using all of your resources. The dramatic use of your voice is one resource; your body is another. Although you are not walking around the stage, you are not motionless either. Your actions will be more natural if you don't plan a particular gesture or facial expression to accompany a certain line.

Rather, you should get so involved in the script that your physical reactions come naturally. Don't think of yourself as a reader of lines; think of yourself as the character from whom the lines would reasonably issue. Understand your motivation, your reasons for doing and saying everything you do and say. Understand your relationships to the other characters and how you react differently to each one. Again, try different approaches. Practice in front of a mirror. Most important, keep yourself open to suggestion from a director or from others who can see what you are doing when you rehearse. That kind of feedback will help you present the most believable character to the audience.

Action, Another Angle of Vision

While the emphasis so far has been on using your voice to enact your understanding of a text, there are times that you may also—or exclusively—use your body. Improvisation, pantomime, and tableaux are three kinds of dramatic actions that can help you understand and convey your understanding of a text.

An *improvisation* is an impromptu creation of a story or character. You don't need to follow a script or memorize anything. Although you may be given a basic situation, you make up the plot and dialogue as you go. Some of the games you played as children were probably improvisations of situations you'd seen on television or read in books.

Pantomime is a kind of improvisation where the emphasis is on action without words. If you have ever played charades you've done a kind of pantomime. Marcel Marceau is probably the most famous classic mime; when he acts, he creates believable characters in believable situations. What he does is a far cry from the game of charades, but it also takes more training than we can deal with here.

A *tableau* is like pantomime with no action. It is a still, living picture of characters in relationship to each other. It's like a snapshot of action, frozen in time, or like the game of statues you may have played as a child. Seeing characters in tableau is an especially helpful way to understand their emotions at significant moments in the story.

As you read the following play, think about where you might add improvisation, pantomime, or tableaux. Some suggestions follow the play, but we encourage you to come up with your own ideas as you read through the lens of a performer. Improvisation could be used wherever you want to add a scene that was not included. Where did the playwright leave out information that you would have liked to have?

Ouida Sebestyen, the author of *Holding Out*, uses pantomime to add another dimension to the story. But how might you use it differently or in other places in the play? How might you use it to understand the characters' motivations? A tableau could be used any time you want to understand or emphasize the characters' emotions.

Holding Out takes place in both the present and the past. As you read this play aloud, in groups or as a whole class, be conscious of the landscape. On one level, this story can happen only in this place. Why? What does that have to do with Valerie and Curtis? What does it matter to us? Be conscious, also, of the power of memory. What role does memory play overall? What role does it play for each of the characters?

Holding Out

Ouida Sebestyen

Characters

CURTIS
VALERIE
INDIANS OF THE MODOC TRIBE

Time

The present, late afternoon on a chilly spring day.

SCENE: *A roadside rest area. One sturdy picnic table with benches and a trash can are the only signs of civilization. Behind them, in the dimmer light, jagged outcroppings of lava rock and clumps of sagebrush stair-step up a desolate slope. A drum is beating softly, almost like the thump of a heart.*

At curtain rise, CURTIS *strides out through the rocks at right. He is sixteen and comfortable being alone. He stumbles on a stone and pushes it out of the trail with a slender branch he is using as a staff. He also carries the thin Park Service booklet he has used on a self-guided hike. He looks around and, because no one is there to see, holds it with his teeth so he can pretend his staff is a rifle. After a few quick shots he climbs up on the table and continues to read, deeply interested. A truck door slams. He stiffens. A few moments later* VALERIE *appears, dressed like him in jeans and sweatshirt, raking her tangled hair. Neither of them takes notice of the drum which slowly fades away.*

VALERIE. Curtis, don't *do* stuff like this to me. I woke up and there I was, parked all by myself in the middle of nowhere, with my feet out the window. '

CURTIS. *(pointing up the slope)* There's a trail up there that makes a loop. So I walked around it, to get the kinks out.

VALERIE. Yeah, tell me about kinks. I feel like the Hunchback of Notre Dame. How long did I sleep?

CURTIS. About six hours.

VALERIE. You're kidding. Nobody can sleep six hours in the cab of a pickup truck and live to tell about it.

CURTIS. Well, I guess you just made medical history.

VALERIE. Where *is* this? Are we still in Oregon?

CURTIS. *(taking a pebble out of his shoe)* No, we've crossed back into California. After you didn't wake up, I thought, What am I supposed to be doing? So I pulled off the highway and stopped here.

VALERIE. Oh, man—no. Not back in California.

CURTIS. What was I supposed to do, with you zonked out? Turn west and drive till we went down in the Pacific, blub, blub, blub?

VALERIE. You could have waked me up, for starters.

CURTIS. *(softening)* I guess. But you'd done nearly all the driving last night, and you looked really pooped. Snoring away like that. I sort of—

VALERIE. I wasn't tired from last night. I was tired from this morning.

CURTIS. Yeah, I know. I saw it. When you came out of your dad's house you looked really different. Your face was white. I thought maybe he'd hit you or something, and that's why you wouldn't say anything when I tried to talk.

VALERIE. No, I just had to—I don't know—get into a little dark space and stay really quiet for awhile. Curled up. Like a snail. And just wait till the shock wore off. Okay?

CURTIS. Hey, you don't have to explain it. I just didn't know what to do, So I just kept on driving and thinking and wondering. One spot up there in the mountains I was screaming along through this snow-storm. In my dad's truck. Oh, man. I never drove in a snowstorm before. So I thought I better stop, for Pete's sake, and hang around here till you joined the world again.

VALERIE. *(looking around)* You didn't pick a really great spot, Curt. This is pretty awful.

CURTIS. I don't know—it's kind of interesting. All this dark, red jagged rock is hardened lava. You know, like Hawaii.

VALERIE. It figures, I go to sleep in a truck and wake up in a lava bed. Couldn't you have stopped in a town? What am I supposed to do for a restroom?

CURTIS. There's one up the trail. Over past that dark bunch of junipers.

VALERIE. Oh, great. It would be. *(She takes a few uncertain steps that bring her back to her starting point.)* Did you read the same thing I did about some kidnapper or hired killer or somebody—

CURTIS. Oh, that? Yeah—he dumped the body in one of these pits. Not out in the bushes where nobody ever goes—no, it's got to be in there where some park service guy can notice it. But I guess maybe he was thinking the quicklime or whatever would dissolve the—

VALERIE. Curtis! Shut up. Just shut up, you're gross. I'm not in any shape for scary stories. Or this weirdo place, whatever it is.

CURTIS. It's a National Monument. So don't put it down—the govern-ment's trying hard to keep weirdo places like this unspoiled for our grandchildren. *(He rethinks.)* Well, not *our* grandchildren . . .

VALERIE. No store, or anything? What do we eat?

CURTIS. We've still got the apples. And potato chips. I can go see what else.

VALERIE. *(uneasily)* Okay. And I guess I can go see if anybody is stashed in the outhouse. *(She starts off again, and turns back.)* Curtis, if I yell, you better come running.

CURTIS. Don't I always? *(His question stops her, and they lock eyes. She jerks around and goes up left through the looming lava shapes. He goes off to the parked truck.)*

[*A* MODOC INDIAN SENTRY *stands up unhurriedly from behind a rock and watches them go. Another sentry rises from his nearby hiding-place. They wear simple rough shirts and pants, and round flat-brimmed hats decorated with feathers. Their faces and hands, their clothing and moccasins, their cartridge belts and long 1870s rifles are shades of gray, as if they were being seen through gauze, or the haze of time. They study the horizon carefully, pointing and nodding to each other. Their movements are slow, almost trance-like with fatigue. They watch with quiet interest as* CURTIS *returns and puts two paper sacks and a can of pop on the table. His gaze goes past them and he starts to read.* VALERIE *comes back and walks past them, unaware.*]

VALERIE. Yuck. Can't they design those things to flush or something? *(She is holding a large feather which she sticks in her hair.)* Boy, talk about primitive.

CURTIS. Beats a bush.

VALERIE. Just barely.

CURTIS. *(noticing the feather)* What's that?

VALERIE. I found it. Some critter got ambushed, I reckon. Oh, great, you found something to drink.

CURTIS. If you don't mind drinking from the same can.

VALERIE. You're really cute, Curt. Here we are, runaways, with a practically stolen truck on our hands, and maybe the police hunting us by now. And your folks yelling, Where's our baby boy! And my mom blaming everybody in sight—and you make it sound like we're on a shy little first date. *(She drinks and hands him the can.)* Hey, you found the cookies. I forgot we saved some. *(She divvies them up.)* I'm starved! Aren't you?

CURTIS. *(gently nudging her toward reality)* Val, this is all the food we've got. And we're running low on gas. We need to talk about what we're doing.

VALERIE. We know what we're doing. We're having a picnic in lava-land. *(She starts to eat an apple from one of the sacks.)*

CURTIS. No, what we're doing is putting off talking about what happened. And what we're going to do *now*. What direction we're going.

VALERIE. Curtis. Give me a break. I'm not ready. It's too soon—it's just too— Eat. Okay?

CURTIS. *(regretfully)* Val, your dad doesn't want you. You've got to go back home.

VALERIE. Back home? What home? *(She forces an airy laugh.)* You mean my mom's apartment where I hang my clothes and step over the bottles? That home?

CURTIS. Whatever you call it, it's the only place you've got to live in.

VALERIE. That's a big lie. I've got the whole world to live in. I can live right here. People live in trucks.

CURTIS. Not in my dad's truck, they don't.

VALERIE. I can get a job and have my own apartment.

CURTIS. On that twenty-five bucks you've got left?

VALERIE. I've got money. I've got another forty I didn't tell you about.

CURTIS. Yeah? Forty that sort of stuck to your fingers while your mom wasn't looking?

VALERIE. Forty I saved! *(She tests other answers.)* I found it. My dad sent it for my birthday.

CURTIS. Okay. Forget it.

VALERIE. If you're in such a hurry to back out, why don't you just get in your daddy's precious pickup and drive off? I don't need this.

CURTIS. Sure you don't. But you needed *me*, Val. You needed the stupid truck to get to Oregon and find your dad, so I took it and got you there. You call that backing out?

VALERIE. Okay! *(She slings an apple core away, just missing him.)* I needed you. I used you. Sue me.

CURTIS. Val—I'm not mad at you! I'm just telling you something. Your dad's not going to take you in. *(He picks up her apple core and puts it in the trash can.)* Listen, you don't have to talk about it till you're ready. But you've got to rethink your plans now. It's not going to be the way you were dreaming it. *(She begins to pace rapidly.)* What are you doing?

VALERIE. Exercising. *(She marches up and down, swinging her arms. CURTIS and the MODOC SENTRIES watch, bemused.)* I'm stiff. I hurt.

CURTIS. Why don't you walk around the trail loop? It's just about half a mile.

VALERIE. Because I want to walk around right here. Okay?

CURTIS. Sure. Forget it. *(He returns to his booklet, refusing to look at her.)*

[An OLD WOMAN in a shawl and a long skirt, gray with time, enters right and brings a small jug to the two SENTRIES. They drink sparingly. When she offers the jug again they shake their heads and go back to their lookout posts. She hobbles off, left, perhaps to others. Neither CURTIS nor VALERIE takes notice.]

VALERIE. *(looking around, still angry but curious)* What's the trail for, anyway? What's up there? It's just flat.

CURTIS. That's what's strange. It looks like a plain old pasture full of sagebrush. From here you can't tell that the lava is all broken up into crevices and ledges and little caves. It's like World War I up there. Full of trenches.

VALERIE. That book's telling about it?

CURTIS. Yeah. They have them up there in a little box by the trail so you can take a self-guided walk.

VALERIE. Trust you to find a book to stick your nose into, even out here in no man's land.

CURTIS. There were people here, once. There were some Indians called Modocs, and they had a war here. Well, more like a siege, I guess you'd say, because about sixty men held off the United States Army for months, holed up in those crevices.

VALERIE. *(forgetting to pace)* What for?

CURTIS. Because all this around here was their homeland. But the white settlers wanted it, and got the government to send the Modocs to live on a reservation with another tribe they didn't like. So they ran away, and when the Army ordered them back, they refused, and gathered up their people here in the lava beds to hold out.

VALERIE. You mean women and little kids and everybody?

CURTIS. Yeah, the old folks. The horses and dogs. Everything they had.

VALERIE. What did they eat?

CURTIS. *(with a shrug)* What they could find, I guess. And there's a lake back over there. They sneaked down to it at first, but toward the last the soldiers cut off their water supply. *(She starts to drink the last of the pop, but hesitates, and impulsively offers it to* CURTIS. *He shakes his head. She drinks thoughtfully, looking around.)*

VALERIE. Why the blazes didn't the Army just let them *have* their stupid hunk of land and save everybody a lot of trouble?

[As she speaks, the two SENTRIES *stand up warily as a small tattered group of* MODOC MEN AND WOMEN *gather between them. Two tall imposing men are obviously rival leaders, unable to agree about something. They mime an argument. Their supporters, anxiously watching, slowly divide into separate sides.]*

CURTIS. Yeah, that's what some people back East wondered. *(He waves the booklet which has given him the story.)* So finally they sent out five people to be, like, a peace committee or something, to try to talk.

[The FIRST LEADER *defends his position passionately, but the* SECOND LEADER *senses weakness in him, and suddenly grabs a women's shawl and drapes it over his rival's head. The* FIRST LEADER, *shocked, throws it off, but he has been called a coward. His followers back away from him.]*

But it turned out the Modocs had broken up into two groups with two chiefs. One chief kept trying to work things out. But the other group just stood up at a meeting and blew away a general and a minister from the peace party. Naturally the Army said, "That does it—not a *general*"—and started lobbing mortar shells into the hideout every fifteen minutes. Like, this is *war*, man—no more shilly-shally stuff.

[In deep anguish the FIRST LEADER *reluctantly agrees with the* SECOND, *who hurries off triumphantly with his men. The little gray crowd melts away. In contrast to* CURTIS's *flippant comment, the* FIRST LEADER *sinks to his knees in despair.]*

VALERIE. *(rubbing her shoulders)* It's cold here. The sun's about to go down, isn't it? How do you suppose they stayed warm in this place?

CURTIS. I guess they had woven mats and things. Blankets. Some of the ledges and little cubbyholes maybe kept off part of the rain and snow. But it must have been hard, surrounded in here. And nothing much to make fires with.

VALERIE. You think we could make a fire?

CURTIS. *(looking around)* I guess it wouldn't hurt. You're supposed to be in a campsite, but it looks like somebody made a fire once, here in these rocks. See if you can find some dead sagebrush or something. *(They leave in opposite directions.)*

[A SHAMAN appears, wearing a gray tunic, his head bound with a white cloth. The SENTRIES give him rapt attention. The broken LEADER, still kneeling, bends his forehead to the ground like someone badly beaten who refuses to fall. The SHAMAN lifts his arms reverently to the sky. One hand holds a medicine stick about four feet long. Feathers, fur, beads, and charms hang from it on a thong. He plants the stick on a rocky ridge, faces the four points of the compass and leaves. CURTIS and VALERIE return with some small dry branches.]

VALERIE. Like this?

CURTIS. Yeah, this might do it, with a little dry grass twisted up to start with. *(He lays a fire and nods toward the tote hanging from her shoulder.)* You got any matches in that bag-lady collection of junk?

VALERIE. You know I don't smoke. Don't you have some in the truck?

CURTIS. Bound to. *(He goes to look. VALERIE turns slowly, her eyes passing over the Modoc leader and the medicine stick. She rubs her arms, still cold.)*

VALERIE. Curtis? *(She kneels to break up some twigs.)* It's eerie out here.

CURTIS. *(returning)* Not one stupid match anywhere. My dad doesn't smoke either, and I guess he just . . . *(He kicks the pile of twigs.)* We're real pioneers, man. *(He hands her a sweater he had brought.)* I found this, though.

VALERIE. I don't need it.

CURTIS. Hey, put it on. You're shivering.

VALERIE. *(laying her feather on the table and pulling the sweater over her head)* You don't have to be nice to me.

CURTIS. *(exasperated)* Was I being nice? Sorry! I keep forgetting myself and doing weird things my parents taught me. It won't happen again, I promise.

VALERIE. *(too serious to play along)* You are nice, Curt. Face it.

CURTIS. And that's what gave you the idea in the first place.

VALERIE. What idea?

CURTIS. The big idea to come on to me like I was suddenly a new invention you couldn't live without.

VALERIE. What are you talking about? You have a really twitchy mind, Curtis. Always cranking corners and throwing people off balance.

CURTIS. You know what I'm talking about. You needed a way to get to Oregon and track down your dad. You didn't have the guts or money to hop a bus and do it yourself. But you didn't mind working *me* over for a couple of weeks till I was ga-ga-gooey enough to steal a truck and head off, any direction you pointed to. You want Oregon? Sure, I'll just go tearing right up the middle of California on this screaming freeway like I know what I'm doing.

VALERIE. You knew what you were doing. Don't try blaming me for that part of it. You wanted to run as bad as I did. You didn't like the way you were living any more than I did.

CURTIS. Nothing was wrong with the way I was living.

VALERIE. That's the whole point, stupid. You've been this nice decent kid with the good grades—forever! You never had a problem because you never made a wave. Curtis, you needed to make a *wave*. A number nine wave, to see if it was going to drown you or if you could ride it in.

CURTIS. Yeah? *(He sits on the table, as far as he can get from her.)* That's really dumb stuff to think.

VALERIE. No, that dumb stuff is the truth. I did use you, Curt—I admit it. But you used me, too. To test yourself. Am I right? This whole trip has been your test. *(He shrugs and twists the empty paper sacks into lumps, unable to meet her eyes. She studies him, her voice going softer.)* Didn't it ever bother you? To *always* do what was expected of you?

CURTIS. *(with difficulty)* Sure. I guess it bothered me. I guess I thought about it, when my folks started planning my life for me, or things like that.

VALERIE. But you didn't do anything about it, Curt.

CURTIS. *(giving his life a long slow look, and almost smiling at its ironies)* Not till now. Not till Miss Valerie V put the whammy on me.

VALERIE. Is that a compliment? *(She sits beside him on the table, moved by his pain.)* You know what made me sad when I first noticed you in school? The way you always seemed like you needed to put yourself down. Just because you were serious and kind and curious about things, and—sort of, you know, in love with life. *Besides* being smart and nice. I couldn't understand that, how you could be all those special things and still always seem like you didn't like who you are.

CURTIS. What's so smart and nice about this mess?

VALERIE. Oh, great, Curt.

[The SENTRIES *stop searching the horizon and lean quietly on their long rifles, curious.]*

I know you don't think taking your dad's truck was a really smart idea. Or selling your watch yesterday to get the radiator fixed. But I—I realize you're here in the lava bed with me and the Murdocks because you wanted to help me be happier. That's nice.

CURTIS. Modocs. Not Murdock. Mo-doc.

VALERIE. *(softly)* Okay. Whatever.

[The SENTRIES *smile at each other. The defeated LEADER gets to his knees and stares into emptiness, perhaps seeing his people's future.]*

CURTIS. I'm sorry the way things turned out for you this morning. Maybe your dad had his reasons for whatever he said, but—man, when you got back to the truck, I thought—the way you looked—I thought he'd socked you in the mouth or something.

VALERIE. You did? No—he didn't lay a finger on me. Not even a hand-shake. I was a real shock to him, I guess. He opens the door and there I am like Hi, I'm Valerie and I've come to live with you, Dad. And his eyes go like, Valerie Who?

CURTIS. Yeah. I guess without any warning like that, what could you ex-pect? But when you went in, what happened?

VALERIE. Nothing. He asked how was I. He said he was just about to leave for work. That's what really got to me the most. When he looked at his watch.

[TWO WOMEN enter and kneel on either side of the LEADER. One hands him a morsel of food. He pushes it away, not angrily but so abruptly that it

falls from her hand. The women crouch constrained until he finally sighs deeply and holds out his hands to them so they can help him rise. They guide him slowly out of sight.]

CURTIS. But when you explained to him. How things were, and all . . .

VALERIE. He said it was a bad idea. He asked if my mom had put me up to it. Then he looked at his watch again. Damn—he could've faked it! He could've pretended he was glad to see me, and really wished I could stay with him but, golly gee, he was just starting a three-year job at the South Pole or something and he'd see me when he got back.

CURTIS. He didn't know how to handle it, Val.

VALERIE. He ought to have tried. It would've helped a lot if I could re-member he tried. Even *I* take the trouble to lie if it'll make things not hurt so much! Couldn't he?

CURTIS. Maybe he thought it would be easier on you if he just said right out you couldn't stay with him.

VALERIE. He didn't even *try*.

CURTIS. You scared him, Val. You made him feel—defensive and stuff.

VALERIE. Why do people get that way? Why can't they sit down and say, Let's talk? Let's listen. Till we understand each other. What the blazes is so hard about that?

CURTIS. I don't know, Val.

[One of the SENTRIES *ventures out to find the morsel of food, picks the twigs off and shares it with his companion. They eat hungrily and lick their fingers as they return to their posts.]*

VALERIE. *(staring into the distance)* It feels so strange. All these years my dad's been out there, like some kind of magic spell I could make. I knew no matter how bad things got, all I had to say was, Hey, I don't have to take this. I can go live with him. And now . . . *(She struggles to keep her voice even.)* All at once there's not any magic to call on anymore.

CURTIS. *(hurting with her)* Maybe he'll feel different some day. Maybe even the fact that you came to him and asked . . .

VALERIE. It's going to snow, isn't it? The sky's so heavy. We're going to be found here frozen to a picnic table, all white and ghosty.

CURTIS. *(briskly, relieved that she has regained control)* Yeah, it feels really strange to be cold, when you stop to think that all this rock that we're walking around on out here was flowing once, red hot, pouring over trees and grass, and nothing could stop it. *(As he speaks he goes off left to the truck and returns with a dark bundle.)* And all these little mountains were cinder cones, and the ashes . . .

VALERIE. *(interrupting)* What's that?

CURTIS. Wrap up in it. You're still shivering.

VALERIE. It's a sleeping bag. *(Shakily she chooses to laugh instead of cry.)* Oh, man, Curt. Just one sleeping bag? You were thinking ahead, weren't you?

CURTIS. *(surprised into defensiveness)* What's that mean? No. Hey, people take sleeping bags. When they go hunting or something. In case they get stranded or something.

VALERIE. In case they get lucky or something. Were you making big plans for us?

CURTIS. I don't know what you mean. Yeah, I do, but—okay. It occurred to me. Just wrap up in it. Things turned out different. Okay?

VALERIE. *(wrapping herself in it gratefully)* Thanks. *(She hunts inside it.)* I've lost one of my earrings.

CURTIS. No. You lost it while you were asleep in the truck. *(He pats his shirt pocket.)* I've got it.

VALERIE. *(studying his face)* Oh. *(She wraps herself tightly again.)* I keep thinking about the children, and the old ones. How hard they had it. When it wasn't their fault. Have you read far enough to know what happened?

CURTIS. *(referring to the booklet)* Well, the siege lasted three or four months, with these sixty guys holding off twelve hundred soldiers. But they were nearly starving, and when they tried to escape to the south over there, they got captured in little groups

VALERIE. Didn't they ever get their homeland?

CURTIS. *(shaking his head)* The settlers got it.

VALERIE. But it's empty. Couldn't they have *shared* it, even?

CURTIS. *(rolling the booklet into a tight cylinder)* I guess not. And the Army figured hanging the leaders would set the right example. So they did.

VALERIE. Oh, man, that's sad. That's so stupid and sad.

CURTIS. It said when the Army came in here, afterwards, they found like
this stick that the medicine man had propped up in the rocks. It
was supposed to give the Indians victory—you know—stop the bul-
lets and all that. Only it hadn't.

VALERIE. Whatever happened to the other Murdocks?

CURTIS. The Mo—I don't know. It didn't say.

VALERIE. *(suddenly bending forward in pain)* Why couldn't he want me,
Curt? Why couldn't he be glad I was his kid and wanted to live with
him? It stinks. *(She begins to cry.)* It really stinks.

CURTIS. Hey, Val. Don't do that. Listen. Hold out. *(He can't even take her hidden hand.)* You've got to just—hold out. Till it gets better.

VALERIE. *(bitterly, still crying)* You figure four months of holding out would
do it, Curt? Like the Murdocks?

CURTIS. They tried, Val. Aren't you glad they tried?

VALERIE. But it wasn't enough.

CURTIS. You tried, too, Val. This morning—

VALERIE. But it didn't help.

CURTIS. Listen to me. I was proud of you this morning, walking up to
your dad's door. You're brave—don't ever forget how brave. And
you're way ahead of the Modocs—they had their troubles a hundred years ago but you're right here—alive, with everything still
ahead for you. *(She grows quiet as he stumbles on, distressed.)* There's
got to be better things out there, and love, and—I wish I was the
one because the way I feel about you—I mean these really deep
feelings—but right now what they're like is—friendship. I don't
know if that means anything to you, but if it does . . .

VALERIE. *(calmly)* You want me to give up.

CURTIS. No. Just go back. And hold out. That's all.

VALERIE. *(testing reality)* Are your folks going to give you hell?

CURTIS. I don't know. Usually they act like, okay, we see your point. So this is scary, because I don't know if they'll be that way. Because this time we're talking really major . . . *(He turns to her with a small proud smile.)* A really major wave. *(She smiles back faintly, giving him the courage to go on.)* You got to remember it's not all your mom's fault either, Val. She's got a right to her own kind of life. I know you think your dad's a real free spirit and all that, but he shouldn't have bailed out on her—he owed you something—

VALERIE. *(holding the truth away)* You know what's funny? All this time I wasn't even thinking about the soldiers. You know? All the soldiers that probably got killed here. Boys from New Jersey or someplace, lying out there on lava rock with bullet holes in them, wondering how their lives turned out so crazy.

CURTIS. Val, if there's maybe times when you need to talk to somebody older than just me, my folks are mostly pretty reasonable. Pretty understanding. Okay?

VALERIE. *(trusting him)* Yeah, Curt. I can tell they must be. It rubbed off on you. *(She stands up and lets the sleeping bag fall.)* I think I want to walk the trail.

CURTIS. You do? Okay. Yeah.

VALERIE. Before it gets too dark.

CURTIS. Okay. Sure. *(He bundles up the sleeping bag in such a burst of gratitude that he breaks one of the ties that holds the bag in a roll.)*

VALERIE. *(hesitating)* Then maybe . . . There's not much point in sitting in the cab of a truck all night in the snow.

CURTIS. *(gladly giving her time)* Well, probably not.

VALERIE. *(with difficulty)* So. We can head back down toward L.A., I guess. It's not like I'm giving up. Or—or settling for just anything. It's just how things are for now. Okay? *(She walks off toward the trail.)*

CURTIS. *(almost reaching toward her)* Okay. It's kind of rough there at first. Go slow. *(She disappears. He stares after her through several moments of silence.)* Val? You okay?

VALERIE'S VOICE. *(from offstage)* Yeah.

CURTIS. *(calling, now)* Don't trip on the rocks, they're sharp. Just take it slow. *(He catches a glimpse of her.)* Hey, you look like a ghost floating along up there.

VALERIE'S VOICE. *(from farther away)* I do? I'm going on around the loop now, Curt. I'll see you.

CURTIS. *(calling)* Yeah. I'll be here.

[He waits, but there is silence. In it, the drum begins to beat again, a deep heartthrob. He turns his head almost as though he hears it and is seeking its source. He draws a deep breath. With the sleeping bag's broken cord he ties together Valerie's feather, the pop can, and his booklet, and attaches the cord to the stick he had used on his hike. He props the stick up on the table with a pile of rocks, and slowly hangs Valerie's earring with the other charms. As he works, MODOCS appear, beginning a slow exodus, burdened with bundles. They pass behind him, gray and spent, the young ones helping the old, the spared ones carrying the wounded.]

CURTIS. *(softly, in an ordinary voice)* Just hold out, Val. Okay? Because you can make it. You can. You're going to. I love you, Val. But that's for later, when there's not so much to fight.

[He gathers up the paper sacks and sleeping bag to stow in the truck and waits, facing the spot where she will reappear. A dwindling line of INDIANS continues to pass in the growing darkness. The two SENTRIES are the last to go. As the drum stops, they glance back at the two medicine sticks standing bravely in the only light that is left.]

CURTAIN

Note: Although this play is a fantasy, the Modocs were real, and their moving story can still be traced in the rocks of the Lava Beds National Monument in the northeast corner of California. Interested readers can write to the Superintendent, Lava Beds National Monument, Box 867, Tulelake, CA 96134. The Visitor's Center there has literature gathered by the Lava Beds Natural History Association, including a booklet called "Captain Jack's Stronghold" (after the Modocs' chief). It contains illustrations from 1873 editions of *Harper's Weekly* and *The Illustrated London News,* which would be a great help in planning a production of this play.

Log Entry 7

1. Jot down your initial responses. What strikes you? What puzzles you? What images remain after you've finished reading? What is your reaction to the characters?

2. Sketch out a floor plan for this play. Where would everything be located? What would the background look like? Would you have

a painted backdrop or a bare stage? What would be the thematic and dramatic effects of your decisions?

3. Reflect, in writing, on the form of the play. How was reading this play different from reading a poem or a short story? Did the form affect your ability to visualize the characters and the setting? In what ways did you read as a viewer? In what ways did you read as a performer?

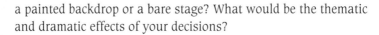Performance

After you have read this play, you might improvise several additional scenes to understand it from different angles.

- A group of three might portray the scene when Curtis arrives home and talks to his parents. How do they react when they first see him? What does Curtis tell them? Do they believe him?

- Another possible scene would be between Curtis and Valerie a month after the events of the play. Have they continued to see each other? How does Valerie feel about her life now? Has Curtis changed at all because of his ride on a "number nine wave"?

- Curtis tells about the Modocs' attempt to save their land and the discussion they had. Using the hints in the play and what you know or can find out about this episode in Native American history, reconstruct the discussion that might have occurred. You will need people to play the parts of the two Modoc leaders, the American general, the minister, and followers for both sides.

You can also capitalize on the use of pantomime in this play.

- As the play opens, Curtis must convey by the way he walks and by his posture that he is comfortable being alone. He has to show his playful, adventurous nature by pretending to shoot a rifle, but he also has to be sure no one is around to see it. He has to react to the sound of the truck door slamming, and he has to show his attitude toward Valerie in the nonverbal way he greets her when she joins him at the table.

- Jot down some notes in your log to help you make decisions about how Curtis will act. Imagine that you are the actor playing Curtis. Write your thoughts as you prepare for this part of your role; use your log to think aloud on paper. As the actor, what can you do to make the audience know Curtis better? How will you walk? How will you greet Valerie? How well do you know her? Will you lean toward her slightly? Are you happy to see her? Are you worried about all the trouble she might have caused for you at home? Are you worried about how she feels?

- The Modocs play a vital role in the play but never speak. How might you portray the seriousness of their condition? Consider their postures, gestures, and facial expressions. As you practice, work with a partner who can tell you what attitude you are expressing through a certain posture. With the feedback of a partner or a student-director and close observation, you can develop a believable pantomime.

Identity, Landscape, and *Holding Out*

As a class, or in small groups, consider the relationship of the play to the themes of this chapter. According to Sebestyen, at least, how do the landscapes of the past—the lava beds and the events that occurred there—affect people in the present? How does she indicate that she believes that past injustices haunt the landscape? Why does she have the Modocs seem oblivious of Valerie and Curtis most but not all of the time? What's the significance of the scenes where the Modocs seem to watch what's happening in the present? According to Sebestyen, how does "holding out" define who we are?

Do you believe that past events influence people and events in the present? Can you think of examples from your own experience or reading?

*L*og Entry 8

Record the key points of your discussion in your log.

*B*uilding Your Course Portfolio

From this chapter, you have a memory poem, your oral collage if you chose to do one, your Readers Theater script and/or videotape of your performance, and other jottings that might be worthy of revising for your portfolio. You might also plan to stage *Holding Out* or prepare it as a second Readers Theater program and videotape that for your portfolio. Remember to include written summaries and reflections for the videotapes and/or live performances.

4

Living Landscapes
of the United States

A remote and expansive landscape like the one used as the setting for *Holding Out* is hard to imagine if you have never seen lava beds or the desert. It's difficult to believe that there are places in the United States where you might drive for hours before encountering other people or finding a town that consists of only four or five buildings. You may be more familiar with concrete sidewalks, high rises, or the artery of a subway system like the one that partially defines New York City. The streets you walk may take you through barrios, tree-lined suburbs, or along the beaches of the Pacific or the Atlantic. If you drive to school, your route may be over twisting mountain roads encased in pine trees, on crowded ribbons of freeway, or across marshlands joined together by bridges. All of these possibilities are reminders of the diversity of landscapes and people in the United States. Each landscape shapes the people who live there, and people shape the landscape they live on.

You'll find layered in this chapter selections by professional and student writers about various landscapes of the United States. You'll write about, photograph, or sketch some of the landscapes that are important to you. You'll consider a variety of angles of vision from which you can extend your ways of seeing and thinking about the landscapes that compose our country. As you did in the second chapter and have continued to do throughout this book, you'll test your perceptions and perspectives by doing fieldwork. We hope that you will come to a deeper understanding of the many landscapes in which you live and those that shape who you are as an individual and who we are as a society. We'll ask you to imagine what future landscapes might be like—those we seem to be creating by our present actions and those that you imagine we will or should create.

*T*he Meaning of "Place"

Much of the literature of the United States depicts remembered or imagined landscapes that make up more than a map's abstract of the plateaus, rivers, mountains, or plains that constitute the geography of a land. The spirit within those physical landscapes, as the ghosts of the Modocs portray in *Holding Out*, is central to what a place means to us. Walt Whitman, one of our early poets, may have been right to suggest in his poem "Our Old Feuillage" that the country was a mosaic of places—from "Florida's green peninsula," "California's golden hills and hollows," "the silver mountains of New Mexico" to "the city wharf, Boston, Philadelphia, Baltimore, Charleston, New Orleans, San Francisco." He goes on to show that the spirit of the vast land grows "out of a thousand diverse contributions." What he describes is a United States of distinct lands and various peoples brought together.

The following poems illustrate how writers can bring together a physical and spiritual depiction of place. Read these poems in one sitting to achieve the mosaic-like effect that we just described.

Driving Montana

Richard Hugo

The day is a woman who loves you. Open.
Deer drink close to the road and magpies
spray from your car. Miles from any town
your radio comes in strong, unlikely
Mozart from Belgrade, rock and roll
from Butte. Whatever the next number,
you want to hear it. Never has your Buick
found this forward a gear. Even
the tuna salad in Reedpoint is good.

Towns arrive ahead of imagined schedule.
Absarokee at one. Or arrive so late—
Silesia at nine—you recreate the day.
Where did you stop along the road
and have fun? Was there a runaway horse?
Did you park at that house, the one
alone in a void of grain, white with green
trim and red fence, where you know you lived
once? You remember the ringing creek,
the soft brown forms of far off bison.
You must have stayed hours, then drove on.
In the motel you know you'd never seen it before.

Tomorrow will open again, the sky wide
as the mouth of a wild girl, friable
clouds you lose yourself to. You are lost
in miles of land without people, without

one fear of being found, in the dash
of rabbits, soar of antelope, swirl
merge and clatter of streams.

#239
Derek Miller

On all of the
highways that you've
never been on
before, you with
your bones of
diamond, marrow
of pulp, a strange
mixture not simply
trees, but something
from someplace where
no hotels have stood,
no guests have been
seen looking as though
they don't know whether
or not they belong.
Your ears of
cleaning rags, your
face a patchwork
of the bandanas of
forgotten outlaws,
the men who never
made it across the
border but died
of thirst in the
desert. Or the men
who made it across
the border, but
picked the wrong
one, and having
burned their bridges
behind them, found that
they did not speak
the language, and

could not change any
of the money that
they had stolen into
currency that would
be accepted, so they
starved. With no
way to even buy so
little as a head of
lettuce, they lay
on park benches under
newspapers until the
print was transferred
onto their skin, and
this you have inherited.
The stories of past
assassinations. I
dream, of an industrial
you, complete with
fire escape and
churning millwheels
visible, smoke pouring
up beneath the bellies
of passing geese, into
the other clouds. You
and the ones who I
wish could be there. I'm
not making plans, because
I don't know what to
expect.

Iowa Spring Viewed from a Plane

Jane Shore

I will not forget how black the earth is!
The grain elevator's sharp momentary 'O'
shifts, leans away and falls
across these squared-off fields.
Occasional roads cut through.
Dot of cow, of car,
no wayward fences here, all order here,

one white farmhouse and a barn and silo
where I can almost smell the corn
going sour, as if the earth were saying
(simply) to me, "Open like these fields."
There is a table, maybe, in that kitchen
where two persons sit who are in love,
perhaps touching, perhaps not, that tension
of distance more exciting than touch;
between them a bowl with one yellow apple,
over which, the wind from the plane I'm in
makes a thin white curtain toss its shadow.

Log Entry 1

- Explain which images in these poems seem vivid or memorable to you and why. Include words or phrases from the poems in your explanations.

- Describe which one of these landscapes is most unlike and then most like any with which you are familiar. Explain why.

- Make a list of any aspect of the landscape that you find in all the poems (for example, color, water, or particular objects). From this list, explain how a description of that aspect may reveal what you think the poet values most in the landscape. Quote examples to make the comparisons specific.

- Describe a place you've visited using detail to make the place vivid and memorable for your reader. Put this description into your writing folder.

Collaborating

With your partner or in a small group:

- Read the poems again out loud.

- Discuss what each of you found vivid or memorable from the three poems. Reread passages that you like and tell why. Talk about ideas or images in the poems that you don't understand and list questions that you can bring to class discussion.

- Compare your explanations of what each poet values in the landscape. For example, does Hugo see buildings in the same way Shore does? Do these poets deal equally with the physical and the spiritual meanings of the places? What specific images, descriptions, or attitudes make you think so? Read passages to each other to illustrate the differences.

- Read the description you wrote or tell about the place you visited. Discuss what you value in the place you described.

Examining the Familiar

Many writers find that the places they know best offer the subject matter they want to write about. Henry David Thoreau noted the importance of Concord, Massachusetts, where he was born and raised, when he described it as an old coat, a morning-robe and a study-gown. Thoreau believed that to know a place you must stand "up to your chin" in it, submerge yourself in what it has to offer, and confront its facts to find the richness. He detailed the homely (gnats, mosquitos, decaying steps) as well as the sublime (clear ponds, babbling brooks, and spring mornings) in the nearly seven thousand pages of journals he wrote. *Walden*, published in 1854, describes the two-year period that he lived alone in a cabin on the shores of Walden Pond. He, like many other writers from the United States, explored the connections between nature and humanity.

Following Thoreau's advice, some of the student writers that we've worked with have submerged themselves and stood up to their chins in the places they know best. Eric Downing was a junior when he wrote the following entry that describes the ranch in Wyoming where he lives.

Other Fences

Eric Downing

Early this morning I watched the calves herded into the range corral for branding. The irons were heated by a sagebrush bonfire to a red hot glow. Inside a smaller pen, Charlie threw each calf to the ground, looping a rope around its back feet and the end was tied to a post. The same process occurred for the front legs until the calf was stretched out, much like the torture rack of the Middle Ages. Each calf would bawl horribly, struggle to get up as the branding iron pressed into its hide. The stench rose and a breeze blew it far overhead.

I remember the first time I was taken to the branding corral. I must have been six years old. My grandpa, J.D., was growing into an old man. He limped along. No man who lives on the range escapes a few broken bones from a battle of wills with the animals. I remember him chewing and spitting and packing more tobacco under his tongue as we walked. The first wave of stench hit me and my stomach turned upside down. For the first time I heard the cry of a calf. I called to my Uncle Charlie to "Stop. Why are you hurting them?" The men all laughed at me and Grandpa squeezed my shoulder with his monstrous hand. "It's okay, son," he said. "It's the way of the range. You'll learn." I was crying by then. The combination of smoke and stench burned my eyes and my uncles and the hired men continued to laugh. I remember vomiting on my Grandpa's shoe and the laughter only echoed away with the wind. Grandpa swept me up in his arms and hugged me close. "Son," he said. "Someday this will all be yours. You'll teach your grandson about branding. Let's get on it." And with that he swept me into the corral and put me next to the fire. "Your job's to keep the fire hot. Stir the logs and keep the irons in the hottest part."

So, today I realized how accustomed I've grown to branding. These calves represent our shelter, our bread, our whole livelihood. The branding makes them legally ours. The brand defends our property much like a good fence does. Yet, a brand's like words shared between people. It's only a symbol of an idea.

Regina Wilson was a senior when she wrote this piece about her neighborhood in New York City.

On the Move
Regina Wilson

He wore running shoes and his dog made insistent whines but clung hard at his heels. A crystal frost hung in the air and must have burned right into the man's lungs. He was running fast and seemed in a hurry to go somewhere. But, that's what it's like in this city. Always in a rush—head down and "mind your own business." As quickly as he'd come into my line of sight he was gone and the path was silent and empty, unusual in New York City to have empty space anywhere. I counted "1,2,3" before five more joggers filled the path, all wearing Walkmans. They ran in unison like their lives depended on precision, their feet hitting the pavement as if they'd practiced some dance step together. Then, they were gone. Around me the City came alive as the clock ticked toward 6:00 A.M.—the screech of tires, the whine of bus brakes, a barking dog, and some preacher-like voice arguing with the air, a siren wails.

I remember how bad I felt the time somebody needed my help, but I kept on moving toward home with my heart beating in my throat. Mr. Malinkowitz owns the deli on the corner in my neighborhood. He's given us kids suckers and gum for free sometimes when we don't have money. He lets us sweep or carry groceries to old Ms. Symonds or something else. Now on this particular day I see this guy swaying, drunk or drugged up or something, and he's shaking his fist at Malinkowitz. I don't know if he's just mad or got robbery on his mind. Anyway, I think if I just walk over that will break things up, but I don't have the nerve. If I just yell someone else will do something. But, I can't. I pick out a man who looks decent and he calls 911 from the corner pay phone. I scram out of there and head home but hear the sirens wail. Later, I don't say anything to Malinkowitz, but he's alive and never lets on if he knew I was chicken.

Suddenly, I'm sitting here in the park thinking about all of this. I feel alone and have the urge to do some running myself. Maybe in a city full of people it is fear that keeps us on the move. It's like some attempt to escape looking anyone straight in the eye.

*Co*llaborating

With your partner or in a small group:

- Discuss your initial responses to Eric's and Regina's descriptions. What do you think is the most important idea each described about the places where they live? In which of these places would you find it more desirable to live? To visit? Explain your answer. In the actual writing of the pieces, what do you think each writer does best?

- Distinguish the different types of information that each paragraph in each piece gives about place. Then explain how these different aspects add to your total understanding of life on the ranch and in New York City.

Modeling as a Way of Shaping a Familiar Subject

Sometimes it is important to get a different perspective or an added dimension of meaning when you are writing about something you know well. Modeling is one way of shaping your subject matter with some guidance from another writer. Use the structure of Eric's and Regina's pieces to structure a piece of your own: In the first paragraph present a description of something going on in the place; in the second paragraph describe a memory of another time in that place; in the third paragraph highlight the significance of something learned from looking at the present and the past together. The first thing you'll need to do is decide which place is important enough to write about, then get the writing started. Choose a place you can observe in the next couple of days.

*W*ork in Progress

1. Write a quick draft that highlights what you think stands out or is most important about this place.

2. Visit the place and write a description about what is going on at the time of your visit.

3. Draft a paragraph that focuses on a memory of this place.

4. Combine the three parts above into a rough draft and add a section on the significance of the place, as Eric and Regina did in their pieces.

*Co*llaborating

- Read your draft to a partner. Have your partner explain what the description reveals about your attitude toward the place you describe.

- Discuss possible revisions that would clarify descriptions, tone, and organization. In future revisions you might find that you structure the piece differently than Eric and Regina did. Modeling their structure was a way of getting started.

- Revise as necessary and include your latest draft in your writing folder. Later you may want to refine this draft for your portfolio.

Exploring the Places Where We Live

The place you chose to describe may or may not have been a part of what you would call your neighborhood. The word *neighborhood* is defined in Webster's dictionary as an "adjoining district and its people; proximity; vicinity." Yet, *neighborly* is defined as "friendly; sociable." We find a difference in tone between these two words. The first word suggests a state of existence—people and place brought together because of their proximity. People who live in the same place are not necessarily connected by feelings. The second word creates an emotional connection, the sociability that is associated with the neighbors. Of course, the friendliness that may or may not exist in neighborhoods is dependent on many factors.

For a moment think back on the pieces written by Eric and Regina. What's a neighborhood for an extensive ranch in Wyoming? Eric explained to his classmates that his closest neighbors are his two uncles and their families. One uncle lives approximately seven miles and the other nine miles from Eric's house. The nearest neighbor who is not a family member lives approximately fifteen miles away. Yet, Eric considers the broad expanse of range land, dotted occasionally with a house, a neighborhood. He said, "Yes, we have neighbors. We see them in town at the church or store. We get together for dinners and dances. People have helped each other build barns or round up stray cattle. Especially in winter, we watch out for each other when the weather is harsh. Of course, family are also neighbors where I come from."

Regina's sense of neighborhood is quite different. "We're all packed in like sardines. In our building (a ten-story apartment building) I meet people I recognize on the elevator or sitting out on the steps in nice weather. I know some by name. What makes us a neighborhood? Well, we share the same stores and streets and elevators. We do make small talk. You know, 'Hello. Nice day. The weather's fine. Your new "do" looks great.' Things like that. Some people have massive families that live in the neighborhood. Others, like us, are just the mamma, papa, and kids. Actually, our storekeepers are the neighbors I know best—like Malinkowitz. He's been here forever. We're protective though. We know outsiders when they come in. Some of the guys who beg on the streets have been here for years, and we know them by name. We're suspicious of strangers. This is mostly a neighborhood of color. The whites, though, who live and work here are trusted. It's good. There's a feeling, but I wouldn't say a closeness."

How would you describe your neighborhood? What do you consider special or unique about where you live? About the people there? How well do you know them? How do you feel about them? All of these questions need to be considered as you think about how you'd define your neighborhood. In what follows, you'll explore your neighborhood in some detail. We hope that you will develop new insights about where you live and that you will write, draw, or photograph your neighborhood as a way of representing it for yourself and others.

*G*raphic

Sketch a map of your neighborhood from a bird's-eye view (like a road map). Label the places that figure most in your life, places where memorable events occurred or where everyday events take place. Identify where the people who are important to you live. If it is helpful, you might create a legend for your map that simplifies ways to represent places, events, people, positive or negative memories, important dates, or any other of the hundreds of ways to depict your neighborhood. At some point we hope these maps will be displayed in your classroom.

Work in Progress

1. Using your map, take a partner on a guided tour of your neighborhood. Point out places that have particular importance. Stop occasionally to tell stories about what happened at certain times or in particular places. Add to your map as you talk. The tour often triggers other memories or significant places or events that you didn't include in the initial sketch. Explain how your neighborhood does or does not shape your attitudes, values, and actions. If your partner lives in the same neighborhood, compare the ways in which you describe it.

2. Write at least three short descriptions of your neighborhood using your map as a guide. Think of these pieces of writing as snapshots—brief, vivid glimpses of people, places, key events, celebrations, or tragedies that have been important in your neighborhood.

3. Display your map (attach your short descriptions) in the classroom. Take some time to examine classmates' maps and read the descriptions they wrote.

4. Include your map and descriptions in your writing folder.

An ode to your neighborhood

Using your map and the descriptions that you wrote, create an "Ode to Your Neighborhood." Although the word *ode* literally means "a lyric poem of exalted tone," we mean it metaphorically as "a song, a celebration" of where you live. Our idea came from the collection of poems by Gary Soto titled *Neighborhood Odes*. Here's one of his odes.

Ode to Los Raspados

Gary Soto

Papá says
>   They were
>   A shiny dime
>   When he was
>   Little, but for me,
>   His daughter
>   With hair that swings

Like jump ropes,
They're free:
Papá drives a truck
Of helados and
Snow cones, the
Music of arrival
Playing block
After block.
It's summer now.
The sun is bright
As a hot dime.
You need five
Shiny ones
For a snow cone:
Strawberry and root beer,
Grape that stains
The mouth with laughter,
Orange that's a tennis ball
Of snow
You could stab
With a red-striped straw.
We have
Green lime
And dark cola,
And we have
An umbrella of five colors.
When the truck stops,
The kids come running,
Some barefoot,
Some in T-shirts
That end at the
Cyclone knot
Of belly buttons,
Some in swimming
Trunks and dripping
Water from a sprinkler
On a brown lawn.
I'm twelve going
On thirteen,
And I know what's what
When it comes to

Snow cones
Packed with the flat
Of a hand and laced
With a gurgle
Of sugary water.
I know the rounds
Of the neighborhood.
I know the kids,
Gina and Ofélia,
Juan and Ananda,
Shorty and Sleepy,
All running
With dimes pressed
To their palms,
Salted from play
Or mowing the lawn.
When they walk away,
The dime of sun
Pays them back
With laughter
And the juice runs
To their elbows,
Sticky summer rain
That sweetens the street.

In this ode, Soto focuses on one specific event in the neighborhood and represents all that takes place through the eyes of one twelve-year-old girl. Yet, we can infer a lot about the neighborhood from how the children are described, the activities in which they engage, and the scant details that hint at what the neighborhood looks like. Reread the poem, looking for clues about the physical place and the people who live there.

Work in Progress

We'd like to stress again that we use the term *ode* in a metaphoric way. In what follows, we've listed a variety of possible ways to present an ode to your neighborhood. Some of you who live in the same neighborhood may want to make this a collaborative project.

If you think of other options or alternatives for collaborating, consult with your teacher to work out a plan.

- Write a poem, memoir, essay, or short story to present a specific portrait of your neighborhood.

- Write a series of vignettes true to the experience of your neighborhood.

- Compile a slide show or film presentation on your neighborhood.

- Write song lyrics and original music. You might choose to combine this option with film or slides.

- Sketch or paint a series of artistic renditions about your neighborhood.

- Photograph your neighborhood and put together a photo essay.

You may have seen photo essays presented in magazines or newspapers. Often a photographer puts together a series of photos so that the combination and sequence tell a story or make a specific point about the subject. For example, one Pulitzer Prize–winning essay was a compilation of photos showing Iowa farmers who had lost their farms. Each photo presented different facets of loss: In one, the family was moving out of its house; in another, an empty barn and a broken-down fence showed the deterioration after a family moved out; in a third, farm equipment was rusting in an open field; in a fourth, a man and woman stood on a hillside overlooking the barren fields. The whole impression was one of abandonment, barrenness, and deterioration.

Collaborating

- Share your ideas with a partner or a small group after you have a skeletal plan for your project. Get help on how to proceed.

- Check with your group periodically as you develop and revise your ode. Consider their advice as you prepare your project for presentation to the class.

*P*erformance

- Present your ode to the class or other classes that may be invited as audience. The combination of these presentations should be another example of the mosaic-like nature of our neighborhoods.

- Determine whether or not your project has potential as a portfolio piece.

*G*etting a Sense of How People Live

You've looked closely at your neighborhood and those of your classmates. We'd like to help you broaden the landscape now and look at neighborhoods beyond those where you live. To start, we'd like to share a journal entry written by John Barker. He spent the summer after his sophomore year in high school traveling throughout the United States. He was part of a group of students that was invited to stay in the homes of other students of the same age. At the time, Barker lived in Nevada. The group hoped to find out more about where other young people lived, how they spent their time, and what they valued. Barker recorded in photographs and video his various impressions of what he saw and heard. He kept a journal and agreed to let us reprint one of the entries. He wrote the following on August 29.

Now that the trip is over and I'm back home, I keep thinking about how much of what I believed about other people wasn't necessarily true. I just didn't and still don't know enough about how other people live and think. I set out to learn about people—what makes them laugh or cry, what they value, and how they live. I was afraid sometimes on this trip when people seemed so different from me. It was always intimidating to walk into a house or apartment and know that I'd live with these people for a week. What if we couldn't communicate? What if they didn't like me? I could relate to Sam, also fifteen, from Minnesota who loves to go fishing in the evening and on Saturdays. No fishing on Sunday. That was church day and the family was strict in observing the day. His father spent time showing me how to cast. I had a bedroom that didn't look much different from home—family pictures, trophies, and plastic flowers. His parents were much like my parents. It was comfortable. We ate corn and hamburgers and mashed potatoes smothered with gravy.

And Sarah. Sarah works at MacDonalds in Tahoe so that she can buy a season pass for skiing. While I was there, her parents invited friends over for a barbecue. I'd never eaten artichokes before. I can't imagine doing it again. Oyster, lobster, and shrimp were piled on trays. I slept on a screened porch overlooking the lake. Everything was clean, including the air, and there were moments I believed nobody but me had ever seen this place before. I felt like I was camping. That's how quiet it was. The house was clean and white and everything shined—no family pictures or heirlooms that I could see. Everything looked new like this was a family starting over. We spent days with Sarah's dad sailing and Sunday came and went without a mention of church.

Then, I arrived at Netta's apartment in Detroit. She lives with her grandmother and five brothers. It was tense. The apartment has one bedroom for the grandmother and youngest children. Everyone else sleeps in the living room. While I was there grandmother Benson slept on the couch. I'm sure she'd spent days cleaning the bedroom. It smelled of Pinesol. I felt lousy about taking her room, but it seemed important to them. I've never smelled such clean sheets before. "Line dried," is what Netta told me. Grandmother Benson had done it "special." Meals were simple and sparse but the family spent hours around the table talking. We'd go out on the steps in front of the building. Walking out, the humidity slapped me in the face like those hot towels you get on transcontinental flights. Children, it seems like hundreds of them, were at play in the streets. People called out greetings, came over to check out the newcomer. The sirens whined continually, but there was excitement and the bustle of life. We went to the Baptist Church on Sunday and I was the only white person there. We sang hymn after hymn and there were barely any dry eyes in the place they get so into the singing.

With Netta it was hard to find common ground for talk until she told me that one of her brothers had been killed on the street only three weeks before. He was just walking along and a stray bullet found him. Netta has this beautiful smile and her eyes look old when they fill with tears. In some strange way we made a connection then. My brother was killed when he was rock climbing three years ago. Once I told her about this, we talked easier about how we felt and our plans for the future.

Collaborating

With your partner or in a small group:

- Compare John's descriptions of the three places he stayed.

- Describe in which one you'd feel most comfortable and most uncomfortable. Why did you make the choices you did? Which of these places is most like your neighborhood? Which one is least like it?

Feeling Alone in the Place Where You Live

Barker learned a good deal about race, ethnicity, religion, leisure-time activities, and family values when he stayed with people from different regions in the United States. He found that the names of people, the places they live, the clothes they wear, the language they use to express ideas, and the foods they eat were very different from his own. As a way of helping you "travel" to other neighborhoods, we've included three writers' descriptions of the places they live.

The following poem was written by Maurice Kenny. Kenny is of Mohawk ancestry. He was born and lived his adolescent life in northern New York state but lived in Brooklyn when he wrote this poem. Kenny has written extensively, publishing more than ten volumes of poetry. Consider, as you read his poem "Going Home," what Kenny said about the poem: "So I travel north to the re-birth of chicory, burdock, tadpoles, otters and the strawberry. I fly with geese who, like myself, have wintered in a more southern clime, or salmon who have matured in the ocean. I travel home to those natal waters. 'Home' is with your people who stand on that earth and partake of its nourishment, spiritual and corporeal (*Between Two Rivers: Selected Poems,* White Pine Press, 1983, p. iii)."

Going Home
Maurice Kenny

The book lay unread in my lap
snow gathered at the window
from Brooklyn it was a long ride
the Greyhound followed the plow
from Syracuse to Watertown
to country cheese and maples
tired rivers and closed paper mills
home to gossipy aunts . . .
their dandelions and pregnant cats . . .
home to cedars and fields of boulders
cold graves under willow and pine
home from Brooklyn to the reservation
that was not home
to songs I could not sing
to dances I could not dance
from Brooklyn bars and ghetto rats
to steaming horses stomping frozen earth
barns and privies lost in blizzards
home to a Nation, Mohawk,
to faces I did not know
and hands which did not recognize me
to names and doors
my father shut

*Co*llaborating

With your partner or in a small group:

- Read phrases aloud that best describe what represents home for Kenny.

- Discuss the details and images in the poem that describe Kenny's attitude toward Brooklyn and "home to a Nation."

- Compare some of the themes that you find in this poem with those you identified in *Holding Out*.

When you think about where you live, are there conditions or circumstances that interfere with or enhance your quality of life? For example, is your home in a high-crime or drug area? In a relatively crime- or drug-free area? How do these factors affect your life? Is noise, air, or chemical pollution a problem? Danny Romero wrote the following story about the neighborhood in Los Angeles where he was born and raised. The place he describes in both the physical and the spiritual setting may seem more like a film than reality. For some of you, the conditions described may be similar to those you face daily.

The Alley

Danny Romero

The setting sun casts a growing shadow over the backs of the wooden houses lining the alley between Seventy-fifth and Seventy-sixth streets. From Bell Avenue it runs east to Crockett Boulevard, across it, then past the grammar school and the Catholic church to Lou Dillon Avenue, then Alameda and the railroad tracks where it dead-ends. The yards adjacent have either fences or walls surrounding them. Some are topped with strands of barbed wire; on others, shards of glass ward off would-be trespassers and felons.

A skinny young boy dressed in baggy khaki pants and an oversize Pendleton shirt scrambles desperately across the debris-strewn asphalt. In his frenzy he almost loses his dark glasses and the woman's purse he has stolen.

Behind him comes Cesar Rojas. Cesar has been walking home from the public library when he hears Mrs. Ramirez's high-pitched voice shrieking, "*Oye cabrón!?* What are you doing!?" At that, Cesar looks over in her direction and sees the young *cholo* stumble for an instant, then regain his footing and head down the alley.

Cesar takes off in pursuit instinctively, not allowing himself time to doubt his actions. Later he will look back on it and see the real trouble he could have been in if he had been led into the alley where the rest of the gang had waited. He runs still carrying a book in his hand. It is a large, hardbound copy of *1984* by George Orwell.

Cesar uses it much as a relay-race runner uses a baton: legs moving in a rhythmic motion, arms pumping the book up and down, pistonlike. Two years earlier, as a sophomore, he had been on the track team, but his lackluster performance had left him feeling a more urgent need to get into college than running in track meets or relay races.

That was the reason he had been spending so much time at the library. His English teacher, J. Smith, had given Cesar a list of books he should read, and *1984* was one of them. Now when Cesar read the newspapers and watched the television news closely, the resemblance between his world and that of the main characters in Orwell's novel grew more apparent and frightening. And he wondered what he could do to make this less true.

Cesar halts in his tracks for a moment. The boy in front of him now comes running back toward Cesar, carrying a long wooden stake. It is more than five feet long and had been used as a means of support for a young tree planted by the city. Cesar backs up. The stake, hurled through the air, flies end over end over end over end over end toward Cesar, then tangles in the electrical wires overhead and falls down, crashing loudly onto the hood of a rusted Volkswagen abandoned in the alley.

The pair cross Crockett Boulevard and pass the grammar school. Cesar still follows the khaki-clad figure.

When he was younger, Cesar and his friends walked this way home from school. Up ahead in the alley, he knows, there is a buzzer at the back door of a garage. As kids, they would press the button, then run off before anyone answered it. Now as he remembers it, he wonders if the buzzer really worked. He had never before waited to see who might answer it.

Plastic bags filled with garbage come flying back at Cesar. The younger boy grabs them as he passes by and flings them backward. Cesar steps over a large watermelon rind and a half-dozen used diapers. The khaki pants stops and picks up a bottle, turns, and throws it. Cesar stops just in time and moves behind a graffiti-covered wall. The glass splinters away from him. The chase continues.

It seems to Cesar like the summer he spent in this alley more than three years ago. It was during that summer before high school when things had changed for him. He was leaving the security of his *barrio* and would have to travel on the bus to another *barrio* for high school. In the beginning of that summer he had felt all alone. None of his old friends was around. And he began to wonder if it was only his family that never went on vacation. Then he met his friends in the alley.

They all walked a thin line between drugs, gangs, and the law. The boys made decisions about right and wrong, for better and for worse. The sheriffs, no matter, always held the boys under suspicion because of the color of their skin and the neighborhood they lived in. And more than once the boys had been lined up with their faces in the asphalt and broken glass. The boys were guilty in the sheriffs' eyes until proven innocent, and sometimes not even then.

Cesar and his friends had still been young enough to build go-carts with washing machine motors, and they raced them over the cracks and bumps in the asphalt of the alley straight away into the night.

After those few summer months Cesar never saw any of those boys again. Except for one whose name was Mando. Cesar had seen him a couple of times on the bus in the morning. They spoke to each other briefly, but they had never been very close among the bunch in the alley that summer. Cesar remembered that Mando once had blamed him for causing him to wreck and flip over the go-cart and break his arm, but they both knew Mando lied.

It had been Frank and his brother Clown who had caused the accident. The brothers, fifteen- and sixteen-year-old gang members, were shot dead at the end of that summer by the sheriffs. Cesar was the passenger on the go-cart that Mando drove, and they both saw clearly the brothers at the far end of the alley, sniffing paint. As Cesar and Mando had sped faster and faster toward Lou Dillon Avenue, the brothers turned with slingshots in their hands and, smiling, fired steel ball bearings. They hit Mando, who lost control of the vehicle, veering closer and closer to a wall on one side, then running into a trash can and flipping over.

The pair crossed Lou Dillon Avenue.

Cesar already can smell the dog turd coming from the Lozano family's yard near Alameda. The yard has been filled with a dozen Chevrolet Impalas from the 1950s and 1960s, sitting among the weeds for as long as Cesar can remember. Many people had offered Mr. Lozano money for the vehicles so they could restore them to their original splendor, but all had been refused.

The horrible smell comes from the chow-chow dogs that guard the yard. There are three or four of them, Cesar does not know for sure. He does know they are the meanest, oldest, and ugliest dogs he has ever met, and he has wished never to see them again. They begin a loud, rasping bark from the other side of the sheet-metal siding that surrounds the yard these days. Another bottle comes sailing past Cesar.

The thief has stopped and is hiding in some shrubbery near the Lozanos' yard. Cesar proceeds with caution. He notices the heavy traffic on Alameda, thousands of cars speeding north and south. He tries to listen for the thief, the sound of his own heart thumping in his ears.

The thief lunges at Cesar from the bushes, this time with a piece of broken bottle in his hand. Cesar quickly raises his book in front of him and deflects the blow. The glass sticks momentarily in the cover of the book, then is twisted free. Cesar slams the spine of the book into the face of the other boy with all his might. The dark glasses go flying. Blood splatters over both boys as Cesar grabs the hand holding the broken glass and turns the wrist until the weapon is dropped. The younger boy pulls Cesar's hair and head backward. Cesar backpedals, knocking both of them to the curb. Cesar turns the boy over.

It is his cousin.

Though it has been years since they have seen each other, Cesar remembers him. Cesar recalls that he is three years older and that their fathers had disowned each other as brothers years earlier after a drunken brawl at a family gathering.

The two boys had never been introduced. By the time they both had been born, the two men were firmly entrenched in their dispute, though it had overlooked the cousins. They knew each other only from those gatherings where the two families had sat on opposite sides of the room and never spoke to or acknowledged the existence of each other. Except for once, Cesar remembers, when at a funeral the two boys had seen each other from across the church and made eye contact, then nodded to each other. Quickly they recovered before anyone else noticed and never let their guard down again.

Lalo is his name, Cesar remembers. Cesar looks into the boy's eyes and sees the growing desperation and almost animal-like look brought on by the pipe that never stops calling. Cesar has seen the same look on the faces of other boys, girls, men, and women in the *barrio* now addicted to rock cocaine. The rockheads, as they are known, always look worried and nervous: tense, as if their jaw were on a spring and wanted to snap right off their face at any moment. Cesar has noticed that at least with the PCP zombies they sometimes look as if they are having a good time.

Cesar unhands the boy and stands. He picks up the purse from the ground nearby. No one has been hurt, he thinks, except for his cousin. He turns back toward the boy and sees the small figure dodging across the traffic on Alameda. Jail will not help the boy, thinks Cesar, though perhaps this chance he is given now might. Cesar can think of no other solution.

*L*og Entry 2

1. Record your initial reactions to the events that take place in the story.

2. Describe any connections you can make between lessons learned in this story and any that you have learned in your own neighborhood.

3. Imagine that the cousin, Lalo, is telling the story. Write out at least one paragraph from his point of view. In your piece keep details of the setting and the events as Cesar describes them.

*C*ollaborating

With your partner or in a small group:

- Share your stories from Lalo's perspective. Talk about the similarities and differences in how each of you perceive his reactions and the type of person you think he is.

- Discuss the events that take place in the story. Explain why you think Cesar did or did not make the right choice in letting Lalo go at the end. What would you have done? Did you find the story believable? Do you think the story is well written? Why or why not?

- Explain whether or not you believe that actions you take in your neighborhood could make a significant difference. If you could change anything in your neighborhood, if you could have three wishes granted, what would you change and why?

*W*ork in Progress

Continue revising the descriptions of your neighborhood that you wrote earlier or draft new ones as the texts you read remind you of other aspects of your neighborhood that you are interested in writing about. You might expand your descriptions into longer scenes that could take the form of personal narratives, poems, or fictional pieces.

The scenes that follow are taken from Ruth Vinz's journal. Through these exploratory drafts she began to capture scenes that might be useful for a fictional story she wanted to write, a process she explains as follows:

> I had this idea about two girls who develop a friendship when they are young. Somehow, I imagine them together for a reunion when they are in college. They decide to take a trip to Nevada and while they are driving, the narrator, Sarah, keeps flashing back on key moments that defined their friendship when they lived in the same neighborhood. I need to write out some of the scenes before I can imagine a structure to bring this together in some blending of the present and of flashback.

Scene 1

Jamie McCaslin's mother was a drunk. I didn't know this when I was seven, and we'd catch a glimpse of her behind closed French doors, draped across the wingback as dinner time moved in. I didn't know this when I was eight, and we found her more and more often in her bedroom when we'd slip into the shade darkened room.

Jamie, in her khaki shorts, says, "All clear, Sarah," putting an arm through the loop of my elbow like she was nudging me across a busy intersection; Jamie's mother under her navy comforter, alcohol strong in the room like a mist, and me tiptoeing across the plush because I need to reach the window seat, feel drawn to the sliver of light that brings sight back to me.

The glint from beneath the shade reflects off her alligator purse tempting me to touch. Jamie whispers, "She's out." Mrs. McCaslin mumbles and shifts under the eiderdown. And I unlatch the gold hooks, and Jamie says, "How much is there? She loses track of change. She'll never know. Go on, Sarah." And that's when I grab at coins I can't distinguish—pennies, nickels, dimes, half-dollars. The latch clicks shut, louder than I like.

Then my mother is saying, "Where do you get the candy, Sarah?" Grandma looks her stern look, eyebrows curve in the wrinkle of brow as she dishes mashed potatoes, whipped in heavy cream, next carrots steamed past crispness. And mother again, in her threatening voice, "Where do you get the money?"

Lord knows we don't have the money and my throat chokes dry for an answer. It is easy to steal quarters from Mrs. McCaslin's purse and head out for Wilson's market for a Fudgesicle, a Butterfinger, or penny Tootsie Rolls. Finally, we take dollar bills then fives to buy Revlon lip ice, Blue Waltz, and roll-on eyeshadow at Woolworth's. We hide our secrets in pockets of cardigan sweaters in my bureau. The drawer fills to bulging while we wait for a day when we dare to wear the sin across our faces. Looking back, this was a time when I thought Jamie's mother was careless or distracted. Now I know, in truth, she was a drunk, pure and simple.

A day comes when I know I must give back all that I have taken: Reverend Grayson looks right at me when he says, "Eye of God, the eye of God, God bends over you, sees every hand twitch, hears the thoughts that pull at your heart; hears the voices in your head; God knows everything; God sees everything." After church, I race to Jamie's: out on the front steps arguing with her; Jamie oblivious to my need for absolutions; her mother staggers through the screen door, camouflaged by shadow, and Jamie talks furiously, her arms flailing. They turn to go inside. Jamie steadies her mother's step as I turn my back and descend the thick, painted stoop bearing a heart near bursting with my need to confess, but Jamie's voice above Reverend Grayson's, the congregation's, or my own, echoes: "She's a drunk, Sarah; it doesn't matter because she's always drunk; Dad says she can't say her own name half the time. She's a drunk, Sarah."

Scene 2

We're breezing across Nevada, and I try to explain to Jamie why I love the emptiness of the desert, the predictability of broken yellow lines that unwind under the wheels. "What's to love," Jamie wants to know, "about dust and sagebrush and the black night?" Yet, it is in the deserts of the West that I first felt myself to be myself, sensing how insignificant were my thefts, and yet how full is the capacity to hope for more in a world that possesses such darkness and space and wind.

The headlights freeze a jackrabbit to numbness. I feel the fur break loose from bone as I hear the thud. This rabbit is beautiful, his brown fur and brilliant white breast, his appalled eyes catching the headlight beam. For now, I wonder if this is the desert's way of getting back at me for discovering its beauty.

"Two hundred fifty miles to clean sheets and sleep," Jamie stretches her legs long to shift weight. Two hundred fifty miles down a road that slithers silvery toward a mirage of city lights on the horizon. "Perspective," Jamie announces as if she's heard my thought. "Remember Mrs. Graywolf?" she's asking. I remember. Mrs. Graywolf taught art. She'd make a desert highway with three quick strokes. A highway that sucked you into its vanishing point. Before me is a mirage of city, a desert river shimmering just out of reach. The road's one quick stroke and Jamie's saying something from *Isaiah* about streams in the desert. Something like: Do not look back; do not ponder things that are past.

Scene 3

What was it I thought about that morning when Mr. McCaslin hoisted the wicker basket in the back of the '52 Ford wagon? I know we filled the basket near bursting with foods I'd never tasted at home—thick slabs of pastrami, french bread, kosher dills, cocktail onions, dijon mustard, and potato chips. Food, I believed, existed only in the McCaslin kitchen. At our house we raised our own meat—chickens and a calf each year; our own vegetables, fresh in summer then stored in the cellar or canned in a kitchen where walls sweated steam for days running. Mason jars, glass lids, my mother and grandmother canning days on end. Other days: huge pots of soup bubbling; bread rising near the pot belly stove; the smell of yeast thick in the air. But, at the McCaslins, I discovered the sweet world of delicacies.

Mrs. McCaslin waves from the kitchen window, her face obscured by the pane of glass. I wonder if she makes a resolution as we back out: "I will not take a drink today. I will stay sober. I will clean the fish and wash the huckleberries when they get back. I will not take a drink." And then she takes one drink. Only one. Then another. By noon she's in the wingback imagining us: three figures darkened by the thick bushes, silver buckets in hand; the groves, a thick lace of green. By early afternoon she opens a new bottle of gin, at the moment Jamie catches her first fish: Mr. McCaslin, arms wrapped around her, both laughing as he helps her reel it in. "Tighten the drag. Not that much. Keep the rod tip up. A little tension on the line. Tighten up now. Yes. Keep the slack out of the line. Don't horse it." Jamie's dancing her little dance—arms tense, hand on the reel, feet in motion. Her back arches, neck muscles taut. Mr. McCaslin leads, a touch here, a touch there. Then, the fish. Mrs. McCaslin searches for more tonic water. Resorts to straight gin.

We search out huckleberries, buried under thick leaves, fill the buckets overfull. By 3:00 we load berries, five rainbow trout in ice, then the four-hour drive down the canyon. Headlights beam shadows into the garage—fishing poles lock into the rack; buckets litter the workbench; the picnic basket comes out, lighter than before. Finally, the ice chest.

We enter the darkening house, full of ourselves, laughing through the re-telling of Jamie's catch. The kitchen light blossoms. We run the flight of stairs. "Mom, Mom, I caught a fish. It's a three pounder! Mom!" Jamie takes two steps with each leap. It is her dance again. I follow breathlessly. Jamie stops short of the second landing. I bump her forward in my hurry to keep up. Her shoulder knocks against the wall with a dull thud as she straddles the rag of a body that was her mother. Between Jamie's legs I see a mouth, lips slightly apart, a pool of drying foam oozing out, but a second pool, rust colored and more recent taking over the first. Jamie screams, "Dad, Dad, I need you. Dad!"

I feel the pastrami, the dijon, the huckleberries rise in my throat. I gag back the sweet day. I want to go home. I want to sleep in my own bed tonight. It is a relief when Mr. McCaslin excuses me, "It's time for you to go home, Sarah. Jamie will call you tomorrow." He reminds me to take a bowl of huckleberries and two trout home. I walk the block alone and forget to tell my family what I've seen.

"How was the day, Sarah?" My mother feeds the last of the whites through the wringer. Grandmother draws a hot bath for me, checking through my hair for ticks. "This time of year the ticks are thick in the canyon. I remember when your Uncle Buddy came home with seven already burrowing into his scalp," she scrubs my hair hard. She tops off the cleaning with rubbing alcohol. "We had to burn those ticks out," she weaves her finger in and out of my hair, checking.

"What prayer will you say tonight, Child?" she asks as she tucks the blanket tight around my neck. I think of nothing to ask God for. I think I hear a lone siren whir to a stop down the street. I imagine the red lights flashing; a stretcher, Mr. McCaslin pale, the ticks burrowing into his scalp as I drift into sleep. Jamie doesn't call the next day. I wait. I can't eat the trout we've cooked for dinner. The huckleberries, placed on rice pudding, turn my stomach. "Are you sick, Sarah?" My mother feels my forehead. "I hope she doesn't have a tick burrowing in," announces my grandmother as she carries the full plate to the kitchen.

Scene 4

The waitress plonks down the coffee cups like she's mad at us for something we've said. She has a right. It's 2:30 A.M. Truckers line Naugahyde stools. There isn't a table in the place, just this counter with discolored Formica and pock marks from cigarette burns. The coffee is bitter. I remember hearing that truck stops have good coffee. It isn't true in Fallon, Nevada. The counter feels gritty against my forearm. I reach for a napkin but the metal dispenser's empty, both sides. Jamie, hand on chin, asks the trucker next to her how much longer it will take us to get to Reno. She's turned on her stool, sideways, toward him, studying the square jaw line and the teeth, dazzlingly white, against his tan.

"Then you'll be heading for San Francisco tomorrow?" I see his hand cradle his chin, mirroring Jamie's gesture. Outside, truck lights send lightning flashes into the night's darkness.

"We better hit the road, Jamie. We've got another two hours to Reno." She does not speak or turn around. The trucker narrows his eyes at me. No one is smiling.

Scene 5

I wonder what terrible thing I have done. The McCaslins drive by me on Elm Street but don't wave. Their eyes fasten to the road ahead. Jamie, sitting in the back seat, studies the back of her father's head. The car crawls forward, slowly. I watch my tanned toes move toward the cracks in the sidewalk ahead of me. I know the car has turned into their driveway when I hear metal against metal as the garage door opens. Then silence. Jamie isn't calling, "Sarah, Sarah, wait up." Mr. McCaslin isn't shouting, "Hey, Sport, you wanna sink a few?" For now, walking the hot pavement home, the tears come, unfolding a blossom of fear or sorrow that I can't understand.

*Co*llaborating

With a partner or in a small group:

- Share your initial impressions.

- Describe what type of person you think Sarah is. What type of person is Mr. McCaslin? Jamie? What makes you think so?

- Jot notes about the relationship between Sarah and Jamie. Why do you think they have maintained a friendship all these years?

- Do you think your family would hide its problems from neighbors? Would you tell your family about neighbors' problems, or would you keep silent as Sarah did? Think of circumstances in which you might or might not reveal such information.

- Review the three selections that you read in this section, Getting a Sense of How People Live, and discuss some of the issues that are raised about what is important to people about the quality of life in their neighborhoods and what conditions exist that work against achieving it. Discuss these issues and think about what each selection suggests that is important to your understanding about how people live.

Performance

- Write a script for a one-scene performance in which some of the characters from the selections come together to describe where they live and what affects their quality of life. You'll need to think of some way to bring them together. It may be outrageous or common. The key is that they have some motivation to get into a discussion about how they live and what is important to them. You might put them together on a talk show, have them meet in an airport or a hospital. Your script may have more characters than the major ones introduced in the text. You may need to create new characters to explain some situations. Create enough roles for the members in your group even if someone serves as narrator or has some other role. You might choose to write a script that depicts your neighborhood or a collection of neighborhoods that are represented by your performance group instead. Assign parts, rehearse, and present these scenarios to the class.

- Write a series of scenarios, either individually or collaboratively. You might choose to illustrate these or transform them into a fictional story or a series of poems.

Portfolio Entry

You might want to consider a video of the performance or final drafts of personal narratives, stories, or poems as portfolio entries.

Traveling the Landscapes

If you've done any traveling throughout the United States, you've probably encountered places where the physical landscape doesn't look anything like where you live. You may have thought about whether you'd like to live there. Maybe the people did or didn't impress you. We carry such impressions away from our travels. Of course, many of our travels may not be actual visits to places. Places you have read about or seen in films or on television are part of a landscape of the United States that you know better than you might have imagined.

Graphic

Draw a map (use extra-large paper) of your version of the landscapes of the United States. You might use an actual map to make the outline or create your own map. Fill in the names of places, names of people, highways, and landmarks that you know and have read or heard about. You might want to label areas with words that describe your feelings about various places. You might use symbols for certain physical or spiritual characteristics. Leave uncharted territory blank, or find ways to depict the blurred vision that you have of places you don't know. You'll think of other ways we haven't mentioned here.

Collaborating

Take a partner on a guided tour. Describe the places you've included and why you depicted them the way you did. You might find that talking about your map with someone triggers other ideas or memories. Your partner's map may give you additional ideas as well. After your discussion, add other places or representations to your map.

Work in Progress

Store your map in your writing folder so that you can make additions as you think of them. You may find that the next few reading selections give you more ideas.

Landscapes from the Past

The map you've drawn may represent the landscape of the United States as it exists today. Did you include any historical events or sites on your map? For example, you might have included the Oregon Trail, sites of battles, important events, and natural or man-made disasters. Obviously there isn't room to put everything on your map, but one way of re-seeing the landscapes of the United States is to imagine how past events and circumstances create a layered map—from the earliest civilizations that inhabited this land to the present moment.

You've probably seen in an encyclopedia or an anatomy textbook a series of anatomical drawings of the human body where layer after layer of transparent plastic, differentiating one body system from another, is added to the human skeleton. We imagine a map of the United States in much the same way. Whether you are studying historical or literary texts, each layer adds a dimension to what we know about the country in which we live. The following poem, written by Leticia Monroe when she was a junior, imagines the past in a place she was visiting. We think that Leticia's poem emphasizes again what we introduced with the play *Holding Out*. Both serve to remind us that the ghosts of landscapes that are layered beneath and over others produce a composite that represents the rich layers of the landscape of the United States.

Monuments
Leticia Monroe

It's like walking into a museum
where stone has been cracked open
to let the spirits walk on earth
again.

Imagine the mother, holding
the dying infant in her arms.
All that's left now:
Lettie Burns Martin
September 7, 1893—September 12, 1894.
What did father say to mother? To
baby Lettie lying too still? Who dug the earth
away, preparer for the box of bone and flesh?

Ernesto Martinez dead at forty-two.
He loved the random joy of dance
and drink and cards. I know it by his name.
Beside him dark-haired girls who listen
now to unheard beats. Ernesto
doesn't come again, he's trapped
in earth so heavy it takes love and memory
to break him free.

Stones grow here like flowers in a garden,
cropping up like weeds too fast, too soon
for those who stand upon the hill shaded
still by maple, birch, and ash.

I pity them the memories I can't sow
for them in life, in love, in constant
competition with the loss. Monuments
of stone so deep I dare not love for
fear of what is lost in love. This
country of monuments has a silent
solace of its own, retreats into the dark
of night, the spade to clink again
another day.

*Lo*g Entry 3

1. Write or sketch your initial reactions to the poem.

2. Use a double-entry log format to record, in the left-hand column, phrases or sentences that are important or interesting to you. In the right-hand column, write your responses.

3. Write about a place you have visited that made you think about past events or reminded you about the multiple layers of land-scapes in the United States.

4. List landscapes or remembered events from your knowledge of history that would make the subject matter for a story or poem.

Collaborating

With your partner or in a small group:

- Discuss Leticia Monroe's poem and the notes you made. Consider any questions you have about the meaning of the poem.

- Read your log entry aloud and then discuss possibilities for revision. If you choose to revise this log entry, you may want to include it in your portfolio.

- Share your lists of historical events and add to your list as you or members of your group think of other events.

Graphic

Add events from the past to your map if this seems appropriate. You might want to think about ways in which you could add layers to the current map.

Learning from the Places We Visit

As you read the following excerpt from William Least Heat Moon's *Blue Highways: A Journey into America,* notice how his attitude is affected by the places he visits. Moon writes that his journey across the United States was his search for "places where change did not mean ruin . . ." He traveled in his van, christened "Ghost Dancing," across back roads from Missouri to North Carolina and on to Louisiana, Texas, and New Mexico. He continued into Utah, California, and Washington state, and on to Maine before returning to Missouri. He discovered a vigorous and imaginative landscape on these back roads, places filled with the spirit of a people who have made this land their home.

Blue Highways: A Journey into America

William Least Heat Moon

Had it not been raining hard that morning on the Livingston square, I never would have learned of Nameless, Tennessee. Waiting for the rain to ease, I lay on my bunk and read the atlas to pass time rather than to see where I might go. In Kentucky were towns with fine names like Boreing, Bear Wallow, Decoy, Subtle, Mud Lick, Mummie, Neon; Belcher was just down the road from Mouthcard, and Minnie only ten miles from Mousie.

I looked at Tennessee, Turtletown eight miles from Ducktown. And also: Peavine, Wheel, Milky Way, Love Joy, Dull, Weakly, Fly, Spot, Miser Station, Only, McBurg, Peeled Chestnut, Clouds, Topsy, Isoline. And the best of all, Nameless. The logic! I was heading east, and Nameless lay forty-five miles west. I decided to go anyway.

The rain stopped, but things looked saturated, even bricks. In Gainesboro, a hill town with a square of businesses around the Jackson County Courthouse, I stopped for directions and breakfast. There is one almost infallible way to find honest food at just prices in blue-highway America: count the wall calendars in a cafe.

> No calendar: Same as an interstate pit stop.
> One calendar: Preprocessed food assembled in New Jersey.
> Two calendars: Only if fish trophies present.
> Three calendars: Can't miss on the farm-boy breakfasts.
> Four calendars: Try the ho-made pie too.
> Five calendars: Keep it under your hat, or they'll franchise.

One time I found a six-calendar cafe in the Ozarks, which served fried chicken, peach pie, and chocolate malts, that left me searching for another ever since. I've never seen a seven-calendar place. But old-time travelers—road men in a day when cars had running boards and lunchroom windows said AIR COOLED in blue letters with icicles dripping from the tops—those travelers have told me the golden legends of seven-calendar cafes.

To the rider of back roads, nothing shows the tone, the voice of a small town more quickly than the breakfast grill or the five-thirty tavern. Much of what the people do and believe and share is evident then. The City Cafe in Gainesboro had three calendars that I could see from the walk. Inside were no interstate refugees with full bladders and empty tanks, no wild-eyed children just released from the glassy cell of a stationwagon backseat, no longhaul truckers talking in CB numbers. There were only townspeople wearing overalls, or catalog-order suits with five-and-dime ties, or uniforms. That is, here were farmers and mill hands, bank clerks, the dry goods merchant, a policeman, and chiropractor's receptionist. Because it was Saturday, there were also mothers and children.

I ordered my standard on-the-road breakfast: two eggs up, hashbrowns, tomato juice. The waitress, whose pale, almost translucent skin shifted hue in the gray light like a thin slice of mother of pearl, brought the food. Next to the eggs was a biscuit with a little yellow Smiley button stuck in it. She said, "You from the North?"

"I guess I am." A Missourian gets used to Southerners thinking him a Yankee, a Northerner considering him a cracker, a Westerner sneering at his effete Easternness, and the Easterner taking him for a cowhand.

"So whata you doin' in the mountains?"

"Talking to people. Taking some pictures. Looking mostly."

"Lookin' for what?"

"A three-calendar cafe that serves Smiley buttons on the biscuits."

"You needed a smile. Tell me really."

"I don't know. Actually, I'm looking for some jam to put on this biscuit now that you've brought one."

She came back with grape jelly. In a land of quince jelly, apple butter, apricot jam, blueberry preserves, pear conserves, and lemon marmalade, you always get grape jelly.

"Whata you lookin' for?"

Like anyone else, I'm embarrassed to eat in front of a watcher, particularly if I'm getting interviewed. "Why don't you have a cup of coffee?"

"Cain't right now. You gonna tell me?"

"I don't know how to describe it to you. Call it harmony."

She waited for something more. "Is that it?" Someone called her to the kitchen. I had managed almost to finish by the time she came back. She sat on the edge of the booth. "I started out in life not likin' anything, but then it grew on me. Maybe that'll happen to you." She watched me spread the jelly. "Saw your van." She watched me eat the biscuit. "You sleep in there?" I told her I did. "I'd love to do that, but I'd be scared spitless."

"I don't mind being scared spitless. Sometimes."

"I'd love to take off cross country. I like to look at different li-
cense plates. But I'd take a dog. You carry a dog?"

"No dogs, no cats, no budgie birds. It's a one-man campaign to
show Americans a person can travel alone without a pet."

"Cain't travel without a dog!"

"I like to do things the hard way."

"Shoot! I'd take me a dog to talk to. And for protection."

"It isn't traveling to cross the country and talk to your pug instead of people along the way. Besides, being alone on the road
makes you ready to meet someone when you stop. You get sociable
traveling alone."

She looked out toward the van again. "Time I get the nerve to
take a trip, gas'll cost five dollars a gallon."

"Could be. My rig might go the way of the steamboat." I remembered why I'd come to Gainesboro. "You know the way to Nameless?"

"Nameless? I've heard of Nameless. Better ask the amlance driver in the corner booth." She pinned the Smiley on my jacket.
"Maybe I'll see you on the road somewhere. His name's Bob, by the
way."

"The ambulance driver?"

"The Smiley. I always name my Smileys—otherwise they all look
alike. I'd talk to him before you go."

"The Smiley?"

"The amlance driver."

And so I went looking for Nameless, Tennessee, with a Smiley
button named Bob.

Collaborating

With your partner or in a small group:

- Describe the ideas, images, or places that are most interesting or
  vivid in this excerpt from *Blue Highways*.

- Reread passages that deal with food, and then discuss the following questions: What does food tell you about people? Give
  examples from your own experiences when the kind and quality

of food helped define the people. What foods are identified with your neighborhood, region, or state? Tell any travel stories from your experiences that are associated with food.

- Speculate on why you think Moon associated the number of calendars with the quality of food. Can you classify the restaurants in your neighborhood or where you've traveled by objects that are displayed on the premises?

- Discuss why you think Moon made this trip. What was he looking for? What does he find? If you travel, what are the major purposes behind your trips? Have you made any startling discoveries about human nature in your travels? What do you think Moon means by "You get sociable traveling alone"?

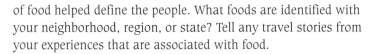

*G*raphic

Add anything to your map that comes to mind after reading Moon. It could be interesting to create another layer that represents your travels if you haven't included those.

Looking at the Landscapes We've Created

When you look closely at the literary landscape that writers have represented or investigated, you'll notice that the subjects they choose are as diverse as the landscapes of this country. They include every kind of person: young, old, rich, poor, decent, and not-so-decent; ethnically, racially, and spiritually diverse; mad and desperate, or loving and compassionate; beautiful and common. The writing includes every landscape: barren, bountiful, desolate, resplendent; enormous, minute, shallow, deep; green, golden, gray, white; mountainous, hilly, flat. Every event is included: birth, death, growing up, marriage, aging. The meaning of the literary landscape is to be found in all the writing, including yours, that we could place layer upon layer across this nation to represent ourselves.

Some writers take their readers for the first time to places they may sometime visit; others create imaginary landscapes; many authors describe how we are changing the landscape by what we've constructed on it. We've become so accustomed to these changes in the landscape that it is hard to imagine that they haven't always existed. As a reminder of how we have changed the landscape, we've included the next two selections. Please read both of them before you write about and discuss them.

Mall Rats

Tyrone Nixon

The rain doesn't mind a rainy day but me and Robert, James, and Joe use one to our advantage. We hit the road, screech the tires, turn a quick right on 105. The mall stands like some circus tent, filled with cubicles of pleasure. We take our pictures first—standing in those booths, grinning like gorillas when the light flashes. A gruesome foursome looking like we own the block. It's ice cream next cause girls in tight pink blouses dip our favorites out—cookie dough with fudge topping and she gives me that smile that shows her tongue and teeth. We stake our claim on a bench near The Wiz and watch the girls go by. Eight billion girls paw through earrings, white blouses, and belts on the bargain tables and there we sit making comments until Russell and Walter come by with some girls they've met who hang on every word. Robert impresses them by striking a book full of matches and then he stomp, stomp, stomps on the flame when everybody's getting nervous and the girls are squealing.

Joe will talk your ear off if you let him, so I head for some peace at the Arcade—red wallpaper, glittering lights, sounds of winning, clinks of quarters—my brain explodes in light. I start thinking that I'm losing my mind with boredom. I head over to the food court and grab a Coke. I see the guys sitting with a girl from school, one of those with finger nails that click, click against the plastic of her cup. Joe's going on about how his brother climbed this mountain in Australia last year and made it sound like he marched straight up this hill and overtook the top. I know his brother nearly died of food poisoning and they had to bring him down on some pieced-together stretcher. I don't say anything cause I'm not trying to impress this girl. Not true, I'm thinking the silent type might be a relief in this place. So she's saying to me now, "Tyrone, what you thinking? You got the downs?" Her eyes are dark as that fudge topping and sparkling with little glitters of light. I'm thinking how I'll ask her out. Tell her she can fix my blues. "Let's blow this place and leave these mutts behind. You and me breezing down 105 with the top down. You and me at the movie. Let's go." It didn't happen. I couldn't get the words out. I sat there like some stone statue in the park and sipped my Coke. She looks back at Joe, "What's with him? Sometimes he's sooo boring." I'm thinking how I'd rather be flying a kite against a strong wind, diving into the surf and feeling the sting of salt water, or shooting hoops with my dad. I say, "Let's go." Above the protests, I hear myself saying, "I'm the driver. I says it's time to go." That's that. We're out of there.

Merritt Parkway
Denise Levertov

As if it were
forever that they move, that we
keep moving—

Under a wan sky where
as the lights went on a star
pierced the haze & now
follows steadily
a constant
above our six lanes
the dreamlike continuum . . .

And the people—ourselves!
the humans from inside the
cars apparent
only at gasoline stops
unsure
eyeing each other

drink coffee hastily at the
slot machines & hurry
back to the cars
vanish
into them forever, to
keep moving—

Houses now & then beyond the
sealed road, the trees / trees, bushes
passing by, passing
   the cars that
     keep moving ahead of
us, past us, pressing behind us
                 and
      over left, those that come
    toward us shining too brightly
moving restlessly
   in six lanes, gliding
north & south, speeding with
a slurred sound—

*Co*llaborating

With your partner or in a small group:

- Discuss other constructions, such as malls and highways, that have sprung up across the physical landscape of the United States.

- Make a list that you can share with the rest of the class. After you've shared the list and discussed it with the class, take another look at your map.

*Gr*aphic

- Add any of the constructed landscapes that you might not have already included on your map if you think these are important. You could add another layer if this seems appropriate.

- Prepare your map for display.

- Display your map in the classroom or share it in a small group.

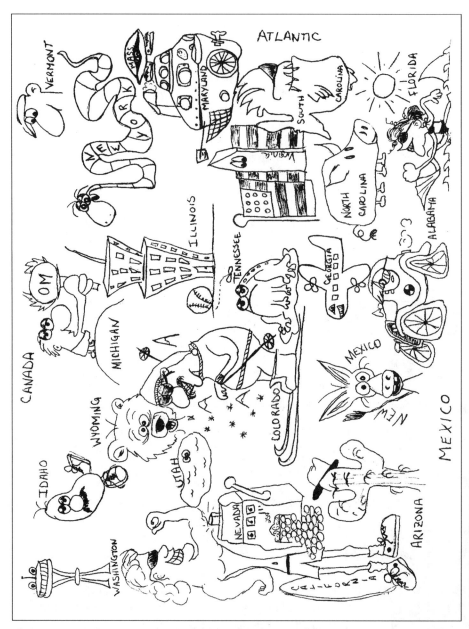

Figure 4-1. *Katie Kress's Portrait of the Land and Its People*

Portraits of the Land and Its People

As a culminating assignment, examine your map for important stories or impressions that you could create in writing, photographs, films, or some other way of presentation. This portrait is much like your ode to the neighborhood except, taken together, all of your class portraits will take you beyond your neighborhood landscapes. To prepare for this assignment, examine your map and determine places, events, or stories that would be most interesting to tell. To give you an example, we've included a map drawn by Katie Kress, a student in Colorado who completed this same assignment (Figure 4-1). Then, we've included her list of possible topics for the "Portrait" assignment.

Here are Katie's notes about her memories of places she's visited over the years or remembers hearing about.

Alabama:	My friend in Alabama wrecked her new BMW.
Arizona:	Cactus grows everywhere.
California:	All guys in California look like the one I drew.
Colorado:	Doesn't everyone come to Colorado for skiing?
Florida:	I got chased right out of the water by a sand shark.
Georgia:	The only place I know in Georgia is the airport.
Idaho:	Isn't that where all potatoes come from?
Illinois:	The only part of Illinois I've seen is the Sears Tower, but I am a loyal White Sox fan.
Maryland:	My friends and I transported a submarine go-cart to Maryland one year for the world finals for Odyssey of the Mind.
Michigan:	World finals for Odyssey of the Mind in Mount Pleasant one year.
Nevada:	Las Vegas, of course.
New Mexico:	In a little town I saw a boy riding a donkey.
New York:	A cute little worm was found on our dinner table trying to catch a scrap or two.
North Carolina:	I ate the best BBQ ribs in North Carolina.
Utah:	Lake Powell is where I learned to water ski.
Vermont:	Mike, one of my friends, lives in Vermont.
Virginia:	Washington Monument
Washington state:	The Space Needle
Wyoming:	Grandpa scared us to death pretending to be a bear, and later that night a real bear showed up.
Tennessee:	My friend's grandpa made it a game to run over all the frogs on the road.
South Carolina:	This is where the fish bit my big toe.

Obviously, Katie's way of cataloging possibilities for a presentation of her portrait may not be the same as yours, but her version is offered as a possibility.

Portfolio Entry

We've listed many of the same options that we did for the ode to your neighborhood. We encourage you to try something other than what you did for that project. If you think of other options or alternatives for collaborating, consult with your teacher to work out a plan.

- Write a poem, memoir, essay, short story, or series of scenarios to present your map portrait.

- Gather a series of photographs true to your travel experiences throughout the United States.

- Compile a slide show or film presentation from your own photographs or from professional presentations.

- Make a collage using magazines or other appropriate materials to demonstrate aspects of the United States landscape.

- Write song lyrics and original music. You might choose to combine this option with film or slides.

- Sketch or paint a series of artistic renditions on your neighborhood.

- Create a photo essay from photos you've taken during your travels.

Collaborating

With your partner or in a small group, share your ideas and get help on how to proceed once you have a tentative plan. Check with your group periodically as you develop and revise your portrait. Consider the group's advice as you prepare your project for presentation to the class.

Performance

1. Present your portrait to the class or other classes that may be invited as audience. The combination of these presentations should be another example of the mosaic-like nature of our physical and spiritual landscapes.

2. Determine whether your project has potential as a portfolio entry.

Landscapes of Possibility

As a final way of exploring the living landscapes of the United States, we'd like to confront some of the tough questions about how we might preserve and extend our landscapes in the future. The film producer Francis Ford Coppola suggested that "we are the custodians of the land. Others have gone before us and someone will follow after us." Of course, as we have tried to suggest throughout this chapter, those landscapes are both physical and spiritual.

What new or different landscapes do you dream of for yourself, your neighborhood, your state, country, and world? How do you think we might go about ensuring the preservation and protection of our landscapes and, at the same time, move into the future? To begin this exploration, we'd like to suggest two of the landscapes that we believe need our attention: the influx of immigrants or visitors to the country and the preservation of natural resources. How we determine to deal with these issues will have impact on the future geographic and spiritual landscapes of this country.

Taking the Familiar Landscapes Away

It's easy to say—and has been said often—that the United States is a land of immigrants. But, as the past few years have shown, the influx of recent immigrants has created more complexity and fewer clear-cut answers about how diverse people will live together. Think, too, how difficult it is for people new to this country to adjust to physical and spiritual landscapes very different from the ones to which they are accustomed. As we consider our future landscapes, this adjustment will be one of the issues that we confront.

You've examined diverse neighborhoods and ways of living, and we hope your examination has made you sympathetic to the situations that people might face when confronted with overwhelming and sudden changes of environment. Imagine that you are getting off an airplane that has landed in a place that is completely unlike where you live. The houses look different; people wear different clothes, listen to different music, and eat foods foreign to you. The language is unfamiliar and the people's values and beliefs are different from your own. Visualize a place that is totally foreign to what you know in your own environment.

*Lo*g Entry 4

Use a double-entry log format and list, in the left-hand column, all of the things that are different about this new place. In the right-hand column, speculate on how you think you might adjust to these differences. What will you do to get along there? How will you know what to do? Where to go? How will you react to the food? What advice or information will you need and how will you get it? Use your own particular strengths to guide you as you write about how you might adjust.

*Co*llaborating

With your partner or in a small group, share your ideas. Agree on a list of ten priorities for surviving in an unfamiliar place.

Read the following excerpt from a writer who describes how it was to enter and try to live in a place unfamiliar to him. In "I Leave South Africa," Mark Mathabane recounts his experiences of arriving in the United States.

I Leave South Africa
Mark Mathabane

The plane landed at Atlanta's International Airport the afternoon of September 17, 1978. I double-checked the name and description of

Dr. Killion's friend who was to meet me. Shortly after the plane came to a standstill at the gate, and I was stashing Dr. Killion's letter into my totebag, I felt a tap on my shoulder, and turning met the steady and unsettling gaze of the Black Muslim.

"Are you from Africa?" he asked as he offered to help me with my luggage.

"Yes." I wondered how he could tell.

"A student?"

"Yes." We were aboard a jumbo jet, almost at the back of it. From the throng in front it was clear that it would be some time before we disembarked, so we fell into conversation. He asked if it was my first time in the United States and I replied that it was. He spoke in a thick American accent.

"Glad to meet you, brother," he said. We shook hands. "My name is Nkwame."

"I'm Mark," I said, somewhat intimidated by his aspect.

"Mark is not African," he said coolly. "What's your African name, brother?"

"Johannes."

"That isn't an African name either."

I was startled by this. How did he know I had an African name? I hardly used it myself because it was an unwritten rule among black youths raised in the ghettos to deny their tribal identity and affiliation, and that denial applied especially to names. But I didn't want to offend this persistent stranger, so I gave it to him. "Thanyani."

"What does it stand for?"

How did he know that my name stood for something? I wondered in amazement. My worst fears were confirmed. Black Americans did indeed possess the sophistication to see through any ruse an African puts up. Then and there I decided to tell nothing but the truth.

"The wise one," I said, and quickly added, "but the interpretation is not meant to be taken literally, sir."

We were now headed out of the plane. He carried my tennis rackets.

"The wise one, heh," he mused. "You Africans sure have a way with names. You know," he went on with great warmth, "one of my nephews is named after a famous African chief. Of the Mandingo tribe, I believe. Ever since I saw 'Roots' I have always wanted to know where my homeland is."

I found this statement baffling for I thought that as an American his homeland was America. I did not know about "Roots."

"Which black college in Atlanta will you be attending, Thanyani?" he asked. "You will be attending a black college, I hope?"

Black colleges? I stared at him. My mind conjured up images of the dismal tribal schools I hated and had left behind in the ghetto. My God, did such schools exist in America?

"No, sir," I stammered. "I won't be attending school in Atlanta. I'm headed for Limestone College in South Carolina."

"Is Limestone a black college?"

"No, sir," I said hastily.

"What a pity," he sighed. "You would be better off at a black college."

I continued staring at him.

He went on. "At a black college," he said with emphasis, "you can meet with your true brothers and sisters. There's so much you can teach them about the true Africa and the struggles of our people over there. And they have a lot to teach you about being black in America. And, you know, there are lots of black colleges in the South."

I nearly fainted at this revelation. Black schools in America? Was I hearing things or what? I almost blurted out that I had attended black schools all my life and wanted to have nothing to do with them. But instead I said, "Limestone College is supposed to be a good college, too, sir. It's integrated."

"That don't mean nothing," he snapped. "Integrated schools are the worst places for black folks. I thought you Africans would have enough brains to know that this integration business in America is a fraud. It ain't good for the black mind and culture. Integration, integration," he railed. "What good has integration done the black man? We've simply become more dependent on the white devil and forgotten how to do things for ourselves. Also, no matter how integrated we become, white folks won't accept us as equals. So why should we break our backs trying to mix with them, heh? To them we will always be niggers."

I was shaken by his outburst. I longed to be gone from him, especially since he had drawn me aside in the corridor leading toward customs. The Black Muslim must have realized that I was a complete stranger to him, that his bitter tone terrified and confused me, for he quickly recollected himself and smiled.

"Well, good luck in your studies, brother," he said, handing me my rackets. "By the way, where in Africa did you say you were from? Nigeria?"

"No, South Africa."

"South what!" he said.

"South Africa," I repeated. "That place with all those terrible race problems. Where black people have no rights and are being murdered every day."

I expected my statement to shock him; instead he calmly said, "You will find a lot of South Africa in this country, brother. Keep your eyes wide open all the time. Never let down your guard or you're dead. And while you're up there in South Carolina, watch out for the Ku Klux Klan. That's their home. And don't you ever believe that integration nonsense."

He left. I wondered what he meant by his warning. I stumbled my way to customs. There was a long queue and when my turn came the white, somber-faced immigration official, with cropped reddish-brown hair, seemed transformed into an Afrikaner bureaucrat. I almost screamed. He demanded my passport. After inspecting it, he asked to see my plane ticket. I handed it to him.

"It's a one-way ticket," he said.

"Yes, sir. I couldn't afford a return ticket," I answered, wondering what could be wrong.

"Under the student visa regulations you're required to have a return ticket," he said icily. "Otherwise how will you get back home? You intend returning home after your studies, don't you?"

"Yes, sir."

"Then you ought to have a return ticket."

I remained silent.

"Do you have relatives or a guardian in America?"

I speedily handed him a letter from Stan Smith, along with several completed immigration forms indicating that he had pledged to be my legal guardian for the duration of my stay in the United States. The immigration official inspected the documents, then left his cubicle and went to consult his superior. I trembled at the thought that I might be denied entry into the United States. But the one-way ticket, which created the impression that I was coming to America for good, was hardly my fault. Having had no money to purchase a ticket of my own, I had depended on the charity of white friends, and I was in no position to insist that they buy me a return ticket. The immigration official came back. He stamped my passport and welcomed me to the United States. I almost fell on my knees and kissed the hallowed ground.

"Welcome to America, Mark," a tall, lean-faced white man greeted me as I came out of customs. It was Dr. Waller.

His kind voice and smiling face, as he introduced himself and asked me if I had a good flight, raised my spirits. As we walked toward the baggage claim area I stared at everything about me with childlike wonder. I scarcely believed I had finally set foot in *the* America. I felt the difference between South Africa and America instantly. The air seemed pervaded with freedom and hope and opportunity. Every object seemed brighter, newer, more modern, fresher, the people appeared better dressed, more intelligent, richer, warmer, happier, and full of energy—despite the profound impersonality of the place.

"I would like to use the lavatory," I told Dr. Waller.

"There should be one over there." He pointed to a sign ahead which read RESTROOMS. "I'll wait for you at the newsstand over there."

When I reached the restroom I found it had the sign MEN in black and white on it. Just before I entered I instinctively scoured the walls to see if I had missed the other more important sign: BLACKS ONLY or WHITES ONLY, but there was none. I hesitated before entering: this freedom was too new, too strange, too unreal, and called for the utmost caution. Despite what I believed about America, there still lingered in the recesses of my mind the terror I had suffered in South Africa when I had inadvertently disobeyed the racial etiquette, like that time in Pretoria when I mistakenly boarded a white bus, and Granny had to grovel before the irate redneck driver, emphatically declare that it was an insanity "not of the normal kind" which had made me commit such a crime, and to appease him proceeded to wipe, with her lovely tribal dress, the steps where I had trod. In such moments of doubt such traumas made me mistrust my instincts. I saw a lanky black American with a mammoth Afro enter and I followed. I relieved myself next to a white man and he didn't die.

The black American washed his hands and began combing his Afro. I gazed at his hair with wonder. In South Africa blacks adored Afros and often incurred great expense cultivating that curious hairdo, in imitation of black Americans. Those who succeeded in giving their naturally crinkly, nappy and matted hair, which they loathed, that buoyant "American" look were showered with praise and considered handsome and "glamorous," as were those who successfully gave it the permanent wave or jerry curl, and bleached their faces white with special creams which affected the pigmentation.

I remember how Uncle Pietrus, on my father's side, a tall, athletic, handsome man who earned slave wages, was never without creams such as Ambi to bleach his face, and regularly wore a meticulously combed Afro greased with Brylcreem. Many in the neighborhood considered him the paragon of manly beauty, and women were swept away by his "American" looks.

From time to time he proudly told me stories of how, in the center of Johannesburg, whites who encountered black men and women with bleached faces, Afros, or straightened hair, and clad in the latest fashion from America often mistook them for black Americans and treated them as honorary whites. A reasonable American accent made the masquerade almost foolproof. So for many blacks there were these incentives to resemble black Americans, to adopt their mannerisms and life-styles. And the so-called Coloureds (mixed race), with their naturally lighter skin and straightened hair, not only frequently took advantage of this deception but often passed for whites. But they were rarely secure in their false identity. And in their desperation to elude discovery and humiliation at being subjected to fraudulent race-determining tests like the pencil test (where the authorities run a pencil through one's hair: if the pencil slides smoothly through, one gets classified white; if it gets tangled, that is "positive" proof of being black), they often adopted racist attitudes toward blacks more virulent than those of the most racist whites.

I had sense enough to disdain the practice of whitening one's skin. I considered it pathetic and demeaning to blacks. As for the companies which manufactured these popular creams, they are insidiously catering to a demand created by over three hundred years of white oppression and domination. During that traumatic time the black man's culture and values were decimated in the name of civilization, and the white man's culture and values, trumpeted as superior, became the standards of intelligence, excellence, and beauty.

I left the bathroom and rejoined Dr. Waller at the newsstand. I found him reading a magazine.

"There's so much to read here," I said, running my eyes over the newspapers, magazines, and books. Interestingly, almost all had white faces on the cover, just as in South Africa.

"Yes," replied Dr. Waller.

I was shocked to see pornography magazines, which are banned in South Africa, prominently displayed. The puritan and Calvinistic religion of the Afrikaners sought to purge South African society of "influences of the devil" and "materials subversive to the state and public morals" by routinely banning and censoring not only books by writers who challenged the status quo, but also publications like *Playboy*.

"So many black people fly in America," I said.

"A plane is like a car to many Americans," said Dr. Waller.

"To many of my people cars are what planes are to Americans."

At the baggage-claim area I saw black and white people constantly rubbing shoulders, animatedly talking to one another, and no one seemed to mind. There were no ubiquitous armed policemen.

"There truly is no apartheid here," I said to myself. "This is indeed the Promised Land."

I felt so happy and relieved that for the first time the tension that went with being black in South Africa left me. I became a new person.

*Lo*g Entry 5

- Record your initial impressions. What are your reactions to the differences that Mark notices at the airport? What strengths does he seem to have for coping? Add to your list in Log Entry 4 any new issues that his account introduces.

- Notice that one of the issues raised in this selection is that people often try to change their heritage—by giving up a name, moving to a new place, bleaching or darkening skin, or changing hairstyles. Recall a time when you tried to hide, give up, or alter something that reflects your background. Write about this incident, describing what you changed or tried to change. Examine why you did what you did. What were the outcomes of this attempt?

*Co*llaborating

With your partner or in a small group:

1. Share your initial impressions, questions, and reactions to this selection. Skim back through the account and find the one or

two most memorable parts of Mark's/Thanyani's conversation with Nkwame. How does this conversation challenge his beliefs about the place he expects America to be? After Mark's/Thanyani's arrival at the airport, are his beliefs supported or challenged?

2. Imagine that you could give Mark/Thanyani one piece of advice before he leaves the airport. What would it be?

3. Make a list of examples of intolerance and prejudice that you think are part of what citizens or immigrants must tolerate.

4. List the accomplishments you think have been made to eliminate various forms of prejudice.

5. What priorities would you set for the next generation for solving issues that will arise?

6. Share your lists and priorities with the rest of the class.

Preserving the Natural Resources

Many writers urge their readers to consider the threats posed to our vanishing resources, wildlife, and various ecological systems. There is a growing concern that we are using or abusing our natural resources and not thinking clearly about how to preserve them for future generations. Whether the cause is to protect wetlands, the spotted owl, a particular gully or range land, or to clean up our water or air, attention is focused on what effect we are having on the environment. In the following essay, Marie De Santis focuses on one such threatened species, the salmon.

Last of the Wild Salmon

Marie De Santis

In a stream so shallow that its full body is no longer submerged in the water, the salmon twists on its side to get a better grip with its tail. Its gillplate is torn, big hunks of skin hang off its sides from collisions with rocks, there are deep gouges in its body, and all around for miles to go there is only the cruelty of more jagged rocks and less and less water to sustain the swim. Surely the animal is dying!

And then the salmon leaps like an arrow shot from a bow; some urge and will and passion ignores the animal body and focuses on the stream.

Of all the extremes of adaptation to the ocean's awful toll on the young, none is more mythic in proportion than the salmon's mighty journey to the mountain streams: a journey that brings life to meet death at a point on a perfect circle, a return through miles of narrowing waters to the exact gravel-bedded streamlet of its birth. A journey to spawning and death, so clear in its resemblance to the migrations of the sperm to the egg as to entwine their meanings in a single reflection.

On every continent of the northern hemisphere, from the temperate zone to the arctic, there is hardly a river that hasn't teemed with the salmon's spawn: the Thames, the Rhine, the rivers of France and Spain, Kamchatka and Siberia, Japan (which alone has more than 200 salmon rivers) and the arctic streams of Greenland. From the Aleutians to Monterey Bay, through the broadest byways to the most rugged and narrow gorge, the salmon have made their way home. There are many journeys for which the salmon endure more than 1000 miles.

As soon as the ice melts on the Yukon, the king salmon enter the river's mouth, and for a month, the fish swim against the current, 50 miles a day for a total of 1500. And like every other salmon on its run, the king salmon fasts completely along the way. In other rivers, salmon scale vertical rocks up to 60 feet high, against hurtling waterfalls.

The salmon gets to spawn once in life, and maybe that's reason enough. The salmon's instinct to return to the place of its birth is so unmodifiable and of such purity as to have inspired hundreds of spiritual rites in as many societies of human beings.

The salmon arrives battered and starved, with a mate chosen along the way, and never has passion seemed less likely from two more wretched-looking beings. But, there in the gravel of the streamlet, the female fans out a nest with the sweep of her powerful tail and the male fends off intruders. The nest done, the two fish lie next to each other suspended in the water over the nest; their bodies quiver with intense vibrations, and simultaneously they throw the eggs and the sperm. Compared with millions of eggs thrown by a cod in a stream, the salmon need throw only 2000 to 5000. Despite the predators and other hazards of the stream, these cold mountain waters are a sanctuary compared with the sea. For the next two or three days, the pair continue nesting and spawning until all the eggs are laid. Then the salmon, whose journey has spanned the ocean and the stream, lies by the nest and dies.

Soon the banks of the streams are stacked with ragged carcasses, and the animals of the woods come down for a feast. The stream lies quiet in the winter's deepening cold. But within a month two black eyes appear through the skin of each egg. And two weeks later, the water is again alive with the pulsing of millions of small fish feeling the first clumsy kicks of their tails. The fingerlings stay for a while, growing on the insects and larvae that have been nurtured by the forest. Then, one day, they realize what that tail is for and begin their descent to the sea, a journey mapped in their genes by the parents they left behind.

The young salmon arrive in the estuary facing the sea, where they linger again and learn to feed on shrimp, small crustaceans and other creatures of the brine. Here, also, their bodies complete an upheaval of internal and external changes that allow them to move on to the saltier sea. These adaptations require such extraordinary body transformations that when the same events occur on the stage of evolution they take millions and millions of years. In the life of the salmon, the changes take place in only a matter of months. One of life's most prohibitive barriers—that between fresh and salt water—is crossed, and the salmon swim back and forth, in and out of the sea, trying it on for size.

Then one day, the youngsters do not return. The stream is only a distant memory drifting further and further back in the wake of time, only different—a memory that will resurrect and demand that its path be retraced.

So accessible is the salmon's life in the stream that more is known about the reproduction of this fish than any other ocean animal. With the ease of placing cameras underwater, there isn't any aspect of this dramatic cycle that hasn't been captured in full color in some of the most spectacular film footage ever made.

But once the salmon enters the sea, the story of its life is a secret as deep and dark as the farthest reaches of the ocean it roams. The human eye with its most sophisticated aids, from satellite to sonar, has never caught more than a glance of the salmon at sea. Extensive tagging programs have been carried out, but they tell us little more than that the salmon is likely to be found anywhere within thousands of miles of its origins, and even this is only a sliver of the picture because the tags are recovered only when the salmon is caught by fishermen, who work solely within the narrow coastal zone. Along with a few other pelagic fishes, like the tuna, that claim vast stretches of sea for their pasture, the salmon's life remains one of the most mysterious on earth.

Collaborating

With your partner or in a small group:

1. Analyze how this one example of the salmon may have larger implications for other environmental issues.

2. Make a list of what each of you believes are the most important environmental issues facing our country or the world in the next generation. Discuss ways in which you think we have begun or should begin to work on some of the issues you include. What do you think are the sources of tension that lead to conflict about how to preserve resources?

3. Research the most controversial environmental issues in your community. Identify sources of conflict and recommended actions. Describe how these local conflicts fit or do not fit into the environmental issues that are most controversial for the entire country.

4. Share your list with the class.

Taking Action

What does the future hold for the United States and the entire globe? We've asked you to examine this question by exploring two of the issues that will be of central concern as we move toward that future. As a culminating project for this unit, you'll have the opportunity to help younger students face some of these same questions and consider how to look at some of the issues that will affect their futures. There are probably many ways that you can reach younger children. One of the most accessible will be through writing and drawing, so we ask that you write a story that raises some issue or combination of issues about the future. You might choose to illustrate your story as well. The readers of your story could be preschool, elementary school, or middle school children. Your story should raise the consciousness of these younger students and help them imagine possibilities or suggest actions to consider as ways to protect future landscapes.

There are many possible ways to present your stories, but you might consider fables, picture books, a short story, or a comic book. Science fiction stories are big winners with middle school children. You have many choices, and this might be a collaborative project. The following steps suggest how you might proceed.

Collaborating

In a small group:

1. Decide which future landscapes you want to present to younger students.

2. Determine the genre for your presentation (that is, picture book, short story, comic book) and the age group of the students you hope to reach through your writing.

3. Discuss possibilities for a story in whatever genre, including setting, plot, characters, conflict, and point of view. In what time period will your story be set? Consider possibilities for illustrations, photographs, or other appropriate art.

4. Have individual members of the group draft versions of the story. Come together for group discussions, work on revisions in a collaborative fashion, and proceed with each section of the story in the same way. Write individually, share, piece together, and fill in details. At times, you may prefer to draft collaboratively and have a group member make notes.

5. Share your early drafts with other groups for revision suggestions. If members of the group have younger brothers or sisters, someone might try out the story on the children and get their

advice. When you are satisfied with revisions, type and illustrate the final version.

6. Send or deliver your stories to an elementary or middle school classroom or library. If you can make arrangements to do so, read your stories to the children in their classrooms. Donate the stories to the class library so other children can read them.

A Future in the Making

In another fifty to one hundred years, what stories will be told about the physical and spiritual landscapes of the United States? What songs will be sung? We'd like to end with two poems that will emphasize the richness and diversity of the places we call home. Our hope is that these two poems will help you reflect on all that you have read, discussed, written about, photographed, or sung during this chapter.

I Hear America Singing
Walt Whitman

I hear America singing, the varied carols I hear,
Those of mechanics, each one singing his as it should be blithe and
    strong.
The carpenter singing his as he measures his plank or beam,
The mason singing his as he makes ready for work, or leaves off work,
The boatman singing what belongs to him in his boat, the deck-
    hand singing on the steamboat deck,

The shoemaker singing as he sits on his bench, the hatter singing
    as he stands,
The wood-cutter's song, the ploughboy's on his way in the morning,
    or at noon intermission or at sundown,
The delicious singing of the mother, or of the young wife at work, or
    of the girl sewing or washing.
Each singing what belongs to him or her and to none else,
The day what belongs to the day—at night their party of young fel-
    lows, robust, friendly,
Singing with open mouths their strong melodious songs.

I, Too

Langston Hughes

I, Too, sing America.
I am the darker brother.
They send me to eat in the kitchen
When company comes,
But I laugh,
And eat well,
And grow strong.

Tomorrow,
I'll sit at the table
When company comes.
Nobody'll dare
Say to me,
"Eat in the kitchen,"
Then.

Besides,
They'll see how beautiful I am
And be ashamed,—

I, too, am America.

Building Your Course Portfolio

Review your various projects or pieces of writing from this chapter
to choose which piece or pieces you want to revise for your portfolio. Refer to Building Your Course Portfolio at the end of Chapter 1
as you work with your teacher and your group to revise and edit
your work.

5

Landscape and Contemplation

*I*n Chapter 1, we asked you to look at a poem from seven angles of vision. These angles, in one way or another, have formed the basis for the reading and writing activities we have suggested throughout this textbook. We now ask you to work through all seven angles as you read and study an essay written by the well-known anthropologist Loren Eiseley.

Reading an essay requires essentially the same processes as reading a poem. However, it often seems different because of the special demands of the essay as well as our own varied purposes for reading this kind of writing.

Angles of Vision on an Essay

The word *literature* generally evokes the idea of poems, stories, novels, and plays; it also includes that very large category we call the *essay*. An essay may be interpretive, persuasive, or argumentative; it may be speculative, meditative, or reflective. Eiseley's "The Star Thrower, from *The Incredible Universe,*" falls into this latter category, but it contains a great deal of scientific information as well.

Because of the complex nature of this essay, we suggest that you keep a double-entry log as you read. Note ideas that you find provocative or interesting; jot down questions, things you don't understand or want to know more about. You may respond with sketches as well as words. Record words or phrases that you like or that you want to go back to later. Don't be intimidated by the number of specialized words Eiseley uses; that's the scientist in him. Above all, don't be too analytical on your first reading. Just read the essay through with an eye toward getting the sense of it and seeing where Eiseley is taking you. You may find it helpful to read the essay several times as you did the poem in Chapter 1.

The Star Thrower
Loren Eiseley

Who is the man walking in the Way?
An eye glaring in the skull.
Seccho

It has ever been my lot, though formally myself a teacher, to be taught surely by none. There are times when I have thought to read lessons in the sky, or in books, or from the behavior of my fellows, but in the end my perceptions have frequently been inadequate or betrayed. Nevertheless, I venture to say that of what man may be I have caught a fugitive glimpse, not among multitudes of men, but along an endless wave-beaten coast at dawn. As always, there is this apparent break, this rift in nature, before the insight comes. The terrible question has to translate itself into an even more terrifying freedom.

If there is any meaning to this book, it began on the beaches of Costabel with just such a leap across an unknown abyss. It began, if I may borrow the expression from a Buddhist sage, with the skull and the eye. I was the skull. I was the inhumanly stripped skeleton without voice, without hope, wandering alone upon the shores of the world. I was devoid of pity, because pity implies hope. There was, in this dessicated skull, only an eye like a pharos light, a beacon, a search beam revolving endlessly in sunless noonday or black night. Ideas like swarms of insects rose to the beam, but the light consumed them. Upon that shore meaning had ceased. There were only the dead skull and the revolving eye. With such an eye, some have said, science looks upon the world. I do not know. I know only that I was the skull of emptiness and the endlessly revolving light without pity.

Once, in a dingy restaurant in the town, I had heard a woman say: "My father reads a goose bone for the weather." A modern primitive, I had thought, a diviner, using a method older than Stonehenge, as old as the arctic forests.

"And where does he do that?" the woman's companion had asked amusedly.

"In Costabel," she answered complacently, "in Costabel." The voice came back and buzzed faintly for a moment in the dark under the revolving eye. It did not make sense, but nothing in Costabel made sense. Perhaps that was why I had finally found myself in Costabel. Perhaps all men are destined at some time to arrive there as I did.

I had come by quite ordinary means, but I was still the skull with the eye. I concealed myself beneath a fisherman's cap and sunglasses, so that I looked like everyone else on the beach. This is the way things are managed in Costabel. It is on the shore that the revolving eye begins its beam and the whispers rise in the empty darkness of the skull.

The beaches of Costabel are littered with the debris of life. Shells are cast up in windrows; a hermit crab, fumbling for a new home in the depths, is tossed naked ashore, where the waiting gulls cut him to pieces. Along the strip of wet sand that marks the ebbing and flowing of the tide death walks hugely and in many forms. Even the torn fragments of green sponge yield bits of scrambling life striving to return to the great mother that had nourished and protected them.

In the end the sea rejects its offspring. They cannot fight their way home through the surf which casts them repeatedly back upon the shore. The tiny breathing pores of starfish are stuffed with sand. The rising sun shrivels the mucilaginous bodies of the unprotected. The seabeach and its endless war are soundless. Nothing screams but the gulls.

In the night, particularly in the tourist season, or during great storms, one can observe another vulturine activity. One can see, in the hour before dawn on the ebb tide, electric torches bobbing like fireflies along the beach. It is the sign of the professional shellers seeking to outrun and anticipate their less aggressive neighbors. A kind of greedy madness sweeps over the competing collectors. After a storm one can see them hurrying along with bundles of gathered starfish, or, toppling and overburdened, clutching bags of living shells whose hidden occupants will be slowly cooked and dissolved in the outdoor kettles provided by the resort hotels for the cleaning of specimens. Following one such episode I met the star thrower.

As soon as the ebb was flowing, as soon as I could make out in the sleeplessness the flashlights on the beach, I arose and dressed in the dark. As I came down the steps to the shore I could hear the deeper rumble of the surf. A gaping hole filled with churning sand had cut sharply into the breakwater. Flying sand as light as powder coated every exposed object like snow. I made my way around the altered edges of the cove and proceeded on my morning walk up the shore. Now and then a stooping figure moved in the gloom or a rain squall swept past me with light pattering steps. There was a faint sense of coming light somewhere behind me in the east.

Soon I began to make out objects, upended timbers, conch shells, sea wrack wrenched from the far-out kelp forests. A pink-clawed crab encased in a green cup of sponge lay sprawling where the waves had tossed him. Long-limbed starfish were strewn everywhere, as though the night sky had showered down. I paused once briefly. A small octopus, its beautiful dark-lensed eyes bleared with sand, gazed up at me from a ragged bundle of tentacles. I hesitated, and touched it briefly with my foot. It was dead. I paced on once more before the spreading whitecaps of the surf.

The shore grew steeper, the sound of the sea heavier and more menacing, as I rounded a bluff into the full blast of the offshore wind. I was away from the shellers now and strode more rapidly over the wet sand that effaced my footprints. Around the next point there might be a refuge from the wind. The sun behind me was pressing upward at the horizon's rim—an ominous red glare amidst the tumbling blackness of the clouds. Ahead of me, over the projecting point, a gigantic rainbow of incredible perfection had sprung shimmering into existence. Somewhere toward its foot I discerned a human figure standing, as it seemed to me, within the rainbow, though unconscious of his position. He was gazing fixedly at something in the sand.

Eventually he stooped and flung the object beyond the breaking surf. I labored toward him over a half mile of uncertain footing. By the time I reached him the rainbow had receded ahead of us, but something of its color still ran hastily in many changing lights across his features. He was starting to kneel again.

In a pool of sand and silt a starfish had thrust its arms up stiffly and was holding its body away from the stifling mud.

"It's still alive," I ventured.

"Yes," he said, and with a quick yet gentle movement he picked up the star and spun it over my head and far out into the sea. It sank in a burst of spume, and the waters roared once more.

"It may live," he said, "if the offshore pull is strong enough." He spoke gently, and across his bronzed worn face the light still came and went in subtly altering colors.

"There are not many come this far," I said, groping in a sudden embarrassment for words. "Do you collect?"

"Only like this," he said softly, gesturing amidst the wreckage of the shore. "And only for the living." He stooped again, oblivious of my curiosity, and skipped another star neatly across the water.

"The stars," he said, "throw well. One can help them."

He looked full at me with a faint question kindling in his eyes, which seemed to take on the far depths of the sea.

"I do not collect," I said uncomfortably, the wind beating at my garments. "Neither the living nor the dead. I gave it up a long time ago. Death is the only successful collector." I could feel the full night blackness in my skull and the terrible eye resuming its indifferent journey. I nodded and walked away, leaving him there upon the dune with that great rainbow ranging up the sky behind him.

I turned as I neared a bend in the coast and saw him toss another star, skimming it skillfully far out over the ravening and tumultuous water. For a moment, in the changing light, the sower appeared magnified, as though casting larger stars upon some greater sea. He had, at any rate, the posture of a god.

But again the eye, the cold world-shriveling eye, began its inevitable circling in my skull. He is a man, I considered sharply, bringing my thought to rest. The star thrower is a man, and death is running more fleet than he along every seabeach in the world.

I adjusted the dark lens of my glasses and, thus disguised, I paced slowly back by the starfish gatherers, past the shell collectors, with their vulgar little spades and the stick-length shelling pincers that eased their elderly backs while they snatched at treasures in the sand. I chose to look full at the steaming kettles in which beautiful voiceless things were being boiled alive. Behind my sunglasses a kind of litany began and refused to die down. *"As I came through the desert thus it was, as I came through the desert."*

In the darkness of my room I lay quiet with the sunglasses removed, but the eye turned and turned. In the desert, an old monk had once advised a traveler, the voices of God and the Devil are scarcely distinguishable. Costabel was a desert. I lay quiet, but my restless hand at the bedside fingered the edge of an invisible abyss. "Certain coasts," the remark of a perceptive writer came back to me, "are set apart for shipwreck." With unerring persistence I had made my way thither.

2

There is a difference in our human outlook, depending on whether we have been born upon level plains, where one step reasonably leads to another, or whether, by contrast, we have spent our lives amidst glacial crevasses and precipitous descents. In the case of the mountaineer, one step does not always lead rationally to another save by a desperate leap over a chasm or by an even more hesitant tiptoeing across precarious snow bridges.

Something about these opposed landscapes has its analogue in the mind of man. Our prehistoric life, one might say, began amidst enforested gloom with the abandonment of the protected instinctive life of nature. We sought, instead, an adventurous existence amidst the crater lands and ice fields of self-generated ideas. Clambering onward, we have slowly made our way out of a maze of isolated peaks into the level plains of science. Here, one step seems definitely to succeed another, the universe appears to take on an imposed order, and the illusions through which mankind has painfully made its way for many centuries have given place to the enormous vistas of past and future time. The encrusted eye in the stone speaks to us of undeviating sunlight; the calculated elliptic of Halley's comet no longer forecasts world disaster. The planet plunges on through a chill void of star years, and there is little or nothing that remains unmeasured.

Nothing, that is, but the mind of man. Since boyhood I had been traveling across the endless co-ordinated realms of science, just as, in the body, I was a plains dweller, accustomed to plodding through distances unbroken by precipices. Now that I come to look back, there was one contingent aspect of that landscape I inhabited whose significance, at the time, escaped me. "Twisters," we called them locally. They were a species of cyclonic, bouncing air funnel that could suddenly loom out of nowhere, crumpling windmills or slashing with devastating fury through country towns. Sometimes, by modest contrast, more harmless varieties known as dust devils might pursue one in a gentle spinning dance for miles. One could see them hesitantly stalking across the alkali flats on a hot day, debating, perhaps, in their tall, rotating columns, whether to ascend and assume more formidable shapes. They were the trickster part of an otherwise pedestrian landscape.

Infrequent though the visitations of these malign creations of the air might be, all prudent homesteaders in those parts had provided themselves with cyclone cellars. In the careless neighborhood in which I grew up, however, we contented ourselves with the queer yarns of cyclonic folklore and the vagaries of weather prophecy. As a boy, aroused by these tales and cherishing a subterranean fondness for caves, I once attempted to dig a storm cellar. Like most such projects this one was never completed. The trickster element in nature, I realize now, had so buffeted my parents that they stoically rejected planning. Unconsciously, they had arrived at the philosophy that foresight merely invited the attention of some baleful intelligence that despised and persecuted the calculating planner. It was not until many years later that I came to realize that a kind of maleficent primordial power persists in the mind as well as in the wandering dust storms of the exterior world.

A hidden dualism that has haunted man since antiquity runs across his religious conceptions as the conflict between good and evil. It persists in the modern world of science under other guises. It becomes chaos versus form or antichaos. Form, since the rise of the evolutionary philosophy, has itself taken on an illusory quality. Our apparent shapes no longer have the stability of a single divine fiat. Instead, they waver and dissolve into the unexpected. We gaze backward into a contracting cone of life until words leave us and all we know is dissolved into the simple circuits of a reptilian brain. Finally, sentience subsides into an animalcule.

Or we revolt and refuse to look deeper, but the void remains. We are rag dolls made out of many ages and skins, changelings who have slept in wood nests or hissed in the uncouth guise of waddling amphibians. We have played such roles for infinitely longer ages than we have been men. Our identity is a dream. We are process, not reality, for reality is an illusion of the daylight—the light of our particular day. In a fortnight, as aeons are measured, we may lie silent in a bed of stone, or, as has happened in the past, be figured in another guise. Two forces struggle perpetually in our bodies: Yam, the old sea dragon of the original Biblical darkness, and, arrayed against him, some wisp of dancing light that would have us linger, wistful, in our human form. "Tarry thou, till I come again"— an old legend survives among us of the admonition given by Jesus to the Wandering Jew. The words are applicable to all of us. Deep-hidden in the human psyche there is a similar injunction no longer having to do with the longevity of the body but, rather, a plea to wait upon some transcendent lesson preparing in the mind itself.

Yet the facts we face seem terrifyingly arrayed against us. It is as if at our backs, masked and demonic, moved the trickster as I have seen his role performed among the remnant of a savage people long ago. It was that of the jokester present at the most devout of ceremonies. This creature never laughed; he never made a sound. Painted in black, he followed silently behind the officiating priest, mimicking, with the added flourish of a little whip, the gestures of the devout one. His timed and stylized posturings conveyed a derision infinitely more formidable than actual laughter.

In modern terms, the dance of contingency, of the indeterminable, outwits us all. The approaching, fateful whirlwind on the plain had mercifully passed me by in youth. In the moment when I had witnessed that fireside performance I knew with surety that primitive man had lived with a dark message. He had acquiesced in the admission into his village of a cosmic messenger. Perhaps the primitives were wiser in the ways of the trickster universe than ourselves; perhaps they knew, as we do not, how to ground or make endurable the lightning.

At all events, I had learned, as I watched that half-understood drama by the leaping fire, why man, even modern man, reads goose bones for the weather of his soul. Afterward I had gone out, a troubled unbeliever, into the night. There was a shadow I could not henceforth shake off, which I knew was posturing and would always posture behind me. That mocking shadow looms over me as I write. It scrawls with a derisive pen and an exaggerated flourish. I know instinctively it will be present to caricature the solemnities of my deathbed. In a quarter of a century it has never spoken.

Black magic, the magic of the primeval chaos, blots out or transmogrifies the true form of things. At the stroke of twelve the princess must flee the banquet or risk discovery in the rags of a kitchen wench; coach reverts to pumpkin. Instability lies at the heart of the world. With uncanny foresight folklore has long toyed symbolically with what the nineteenth century was to proclaim a reality, namely, that form is an illusion of the time dimension, that the magic flight of the pursued hero or heroine through frog-skin and wolf coat has been, and will continue to be, the flight of all men.

Goethe's genius sensed, well before the publication of the *Origin of Species*, the thesis and antithesis that epitomize the eternal struggle of the immediate species against its dissolution into something other: in modern terms, fish into reptile, ape into man. The power to change is both creative and destructive—a sinister gift, which, unrestricted, leads onward toward the formless and inchoate void of the possible. This force can only be counterbalanced by an equal impulse toward specificity. Form, once arisen, clings to its identity. Each species and each individual holds tenaciously to its present nature. Each strives to contain the creative and abolishing maelstrom that pours unseen through the generations. The past vanishes; the present momentarily persists; the future is potential only. In this specious present of the real, life struggles to maintain every manifestation, every individuality, that exists. In the end, life always fails, but the amorphous hurrying stream is held and diverted into new organic vessels in which form persists, though the form may not be that of yesterday.

The evolutionists, piercing beneath the show of momentary stability, discovered, hidden in rudimentary organs, the discarded rubbish of the past. They detected the reptile under the lifted feathers of the bird, the lost terrestrial limbs dwindling beneath the blubber of the giant cetaceans. They saw life rushing outward from an unknown center, just as today the astronomer senses the galaxies fleeing into the infinity of darkness. As the spinning galactic clouds hurl stars and worlds across the night, so life, equally impelled by the centrifugal powers lurking in the germ cell, scatters the splintered radiance of consciousness and sends it prowling and contending through the thickets of the world.

All this devious, tattered way was exposed to the ceaselessly turning eye within the skull that lay hidden upon the bed in Costabel. Slowly that eye grew conscious of another eye that searched it with equal penetration from the shadows of the room. It may have been a projection from the mind within the skull, but the eye was, nevertheless, exteriorized and haunting. It began as something glaucous and blind beneath a web of clinging algae. It altered suddenly and became the sand-smeared eye of the dead cephalopod I had encountered upon the beach. The transformations became more rapid with the concentration of my attention, and they became more formidable. There was the beaten, bloodshot eye of an animal from somewhere within my childhood experience. Finally, there was an eye that seemed torn from a photograph, but that looked through me as though it had already raced in vision up to the steep edge of nothingness and absorbed whatever terror lay in that abyss. I sank back again upon my cot and buried my head in the pillow. I knew the eye and the circumstance and the question. It was my mother. She was long dead, and the way backward was lost.

3

Now it may be asked, upon the coasts that invite shipwreck, why the ships should come, just as we may ask the man who pursues knowledge why he should be left with a revolving search beam in the head whose light falls only upon disaster or the flotsam of the shore. There is an answer, but its way is not across the level plains of science, for the science of remote abysses no longer shelters man.

Instead, it reveals him in vaporous metamorphic succession as the homeless and unspecified one, the creature of the magic flight.

Long ago, when the future was just a simple tomorrow, men had cast intricately carved game counters to determine its course, or they had traced with a grimy finger the cracks on the burnt shoulder blade of a hare. It was a prophecy of tomorrow's hunt, just as was the old farmer's anachronistic reading of the weather from the signs on the breastbone of a goose. Such quaint almanacs of nature's intent had sufficed mankind since antiquity. They would do so no longer, nor would formal apologies to the souls of the game men hunted. The hunters had come, at last, beyond the satisfying supernatural world that had always surrounded the little village, into a place of homeless frontiers and precipitous edges, the indescribable world of the natural. Here tools increasingly revenged themselves upon their creators and tomorrow became unmanageable. Man had come in his journeying to a region of terrible freedoms.

It was a place of no traditional shelter, save those erected with the aid of tools, which had also begun to achieve a revolutionary independence from their masters. Their ways had grown secretive and incalculable. Science, more powerful than the magical questions that might be addressed by a shaman to a burnt shoulder blade, could create these tools but had not succeeded in controlling their ambivalent nature. Moreover, they responded all too readily to that urge for tampering and dissolution which is part of our primate heritage.

We had been safe in the enchanted forest only because of our weakness. When the powers of that gloomy region were given to us, immediately, as in a witch's house, things began to fly about unbidden. The tools, if not science itself, were linked intangibly to the subconscious poltergeist aspect of man's nature. The closer man and the natural world drew together, the more erratic became the behavior of each. Huge shadows leaped triumphantly after every blinding illumination. It was a magnified but clearly recognizable version of the black trickster's antics behind the solemn backs of the priesthood. Here, there was one difference. The shadows had passed out of all human semblance; no societal ritual safely contained their posturings, as in the warning dance of the trickster. Instead, unseen by many because it was so gigantically real, the multiplied darkness threatened to submerge the carriers of the light.

Darwin, Einstein, and Freud might be said to have released the shadows. Yet man had already entered the perilous domain that henceforth would contain his destiny. Four hundred years ago Francis Bacon had already anticipated its dual nature. The individuals do not matter. If they had not made their discoveries, others would have surely done so. They were good men, and they came as enlighteners of mankind. The tragedy was only that at their backs the ritual figure with the whip was invisible. There was no longer anything to subdue the pride of man. The world had been laid under the heavy spell of the natural; henceforth, it would be ordered by man.

Humanity was suddenly entranced by light and fancied it reflected light. Progress was its watchword, and for a time the shadows seemed to recede. Only a few guessed that the retreat of darkness presaged the emergence of an entirely new and less tangible terror. Things, in the words of G. K. Chesterton, were to grow incalculable by being calculated. Man's powers were finite; the forces he had released in nature recognized no such limitations. They were the irrevocable monsters conjured up by a completely amateur sorcerer.

But what, we may ask, was the nature of the first discoveries that now threaten to induce disaster? Preeminent among them was, of course, the perception to which we have already referred: the discovery of the interlinked and evolving web of life. The great Victorian biologists saw, and yet refused to see, the war between form and formlessness, chaos and antichaos, which the poet Goethe had sensed contesting beneath the smiling surface of nature. "The dangerous gift from above," he had termed it, with uneasy foresight.

By contrast, Darwin, the prime student of the struggle for existence, sought to visualize in a tangled bank of leaves the silent and insatiable war of nature. Still, he could imply with a veiled complacency that man might "with some confidence" look forward to a secure future "of inappreciable length." This he could do upon the same page in the *Origin of Species* where he observes that "of the species now living very few will transmit progeny to a far distant futurity." The contradiction escaped him; he did not wish to see it. Darwin, in addition, saw life as a purely selfish struggle, in which nothing is modified for the good of another species without being directly advantageous to its associated form.

If, he contended, one part of any single species had been formed for the exclusive good of another, "it would annihilate my theory." Powerfully documented and enhanced though the statement has become, famine, war, and death are not the sole instruments biologists today would accept as the means toward that perfection of which Darwin spoke. The subject is subtle and intricate, however, and one facet of it must be reserved for another chapter. Let it suffice to say here that the sign of the dark cave and the club became so firmly fixed in human thinking that in our time it has been invoked as signifying man's true image in books selling in the hundreds of thousands.

From the thesis and antithesis contained in Darwinism we come to Freud. The public knows that, like Darwin, the master of the inner world took the secure, stable, and sunlit province of the mind and revealed it as a place of contending furies. Ghostly transformations, flitting night shadows, misshapen changelings existed there, as real as anything that haunted the natural universe of Darwin. For this reason, appropriately, I had come as the skull and the eye to Costabel—the coast demanding shipwreck. Why else had I remembered the phrase, except for a dark impulse toward destruction lurking somewhere in the subconscious? I lay on the bed while the agonized eye in the remembered photograph persisted at the back of my closed lids.

It had begun when, after years of separation, I had gone dutifully home to a house from which the final occupant had departed. In a musty attic—among old trunks, a broken aquarium, and a dusty heap of fossil shells collected in childhood—I found a satchel. The satchel was already a shabby antique, in whose depths I turned up a jackknife and a "rat" of hair such as women wore at the beginning of the century. Beneath these lay a pile of old photographs and a note—two notes, rather, evidently dropped into the bag at different times. Each, in a thin, ornate hand, reiterated a single message that the writer had believed important. "This satchel belongs to my son, Loren Eiseley." It was the last message. I recognized the trivia. The jackknife I had carried in childhood. The rat of hair had belonged to my mother, and there were also two incredibly pointed slippers that looked as though they had been intended for a formal ball, to which I knew well my mother would never in her life have been invited. I undid the rotted string around the studio portraits.

Mostly they consisted of stiff, upright bearded men and heavily clothed women equally bound to the formalities and ritual that attended upon the photography of an earlier generation. No names identified the pictures, although here and there a reminiscent family trait seemed faintly evident. Finally I came upon a less formal photograph, taken in the eighties of the last century. Again no names identified the people, but a commercial stamp upon the back identified the place: Dyersville, Iowa. I had never been in that country town, but I knew at once it was my mother's birthplace.

Dyersville, the thought flashed through my mind, making the connection now for the first time: the dire place. I recognized at once the two sisters at the edge of the photograph, the younger clinging reluctantly to the older. Six years old, I thought, turning momentarily away from the younger child's face. Here it began, her pain and mine. The eyes in the photograph were already remote and shadowed by some inner turmoil. The poise of the body was already that of one miserably departing the peripheries of the human estate. The gaze was mutely clairvoyant and lonely. It was the gaze of a child who knew unbearable difference and impending isolation.

I dropped the notes and pictures once more into the bag. The last message had come from Dyersville: "my son." The child in the photograph had survived to be an ill-taught prairie artist. She had been deaf. All her life she had walked the precipice of mental breakdown. Here on this faded porch it had begun—the long crucifixion of life. I slipped downstairs and out of the house. I walked for miles through the streets.

Now at Costabel I put on the sunglasses once more, but the face from the torn photograph persisted behind them. It was as though I, as man, was being asked to confront, in all its overbearing weight, the universe itself. "Love not the world," the Biblical injunction runs, "neither the things that are in the world." The revolving beam in my mind had stopped, and the insect whisperings of the intellect. There was, at last, an utter stillness, a waiting as though for a cosmic judgment. The eye, the torn eye, considered me.

"But I *do* love the world," I whispered to a waiting presence in the empty room. "I love its small ones, the things beaten in the strangling surf, the bird, singing, which flies and falls and is not seen again." I choked and said, with the torn eye still upon me, "I love the lost ones, the failures of the world." It was like the renunciation of my scientific heritage. The torn eye surveyed me sadly and was gone. I had come full upon one of the last great rifts in nature, and the merciless beam no longer was in traverse around my skull.

But no, it was not a rift but a joining: the expression of love projected beyond the species boundary by a creature born of Darwinian struggle, in the silent war under the tangled bank. "There is no boon in nature," one of the new philosophers had written harshly in the first years of the industrial cities. Nevertheless, through war and famine and death, a sparse mercy had persisted, like a mutation whose time had not yet come. I had seen the star thrower cross that rift and, in so doing, he had reasserted the human right to define his own frontier. He had moved to the utmost edge of natural being, if not across its boundaries. It was as though at some point the supernatural had touched hesitantly, for an instant, upon the natural.

Out of the depths of a seemingly empty universe had grown an eye, like the eye in my room, but an eye on a vastly larger scale. It looked out upon what I can only call itself. It searched the skies and it searched the depths of being. In the shape of man it had ascended like a vaporous emanation from the depths of night. The nothing had miraculously gazed upon the nothing and was not content. It was an intrusion into, or a projection out of, nature for which no precedent existed. The act was, in short, an assertion of value arisen from the domain of absolute zero. A little whirlwind of commingling molecules had succeeded in confronting its own universe.

Here, at last, was the rift that lay beyond Darwin's tangled bank. For a creature, arisen from the bank and born of its contentions, had stretched out its hand in pity. Some ancient, inexhaustible, and patient intelligence, lying dispersed in the planetary fields of force or amidst the inconceivable cold of interstellar space, had chosen to endow its desolation with an apparition as mysterious as itself. The fate of man is to be the ever recurrent, reproachful Eye floating upon night and solitude. The world cannot be said to exist save by the interposition of that inward eye—an eye various and not under the restraints to be apprehended from what is vulgarly called the natural.

I had been unbelieving. I had walked away from the star thrower in the hardened indifference of maturity. But thought mediated by the eye is one of nature's infinite disguises. Belatedly, I arose with a solitary mission. I set forth in an effort to find the star thrower.

4

Man is himself, like the universe he inhabits, like the demoniacal stirrings of the ooze from which he sprang, a tale of desolations. He walks in his mind from birth to death the long resounding shores of endless disillusionment. Finally, the commitment to life departs or turns to bitterness. But out of such desolation emerges the awesome freedom to choose—to choose beyond the narrowly circumscribed circle that delimits the animal being. In that widening ring of human choice, chaos and order renew their symbolic struggle in the role of titans. They contend for the destiny of a world.

Somewhere far up the coast wandered the star thrower beneath his rainbow. Our exchange had been brief because upon that coast I had learned that men who ventured out at dawn resented others in the greediness of their compulsive collecting. I had also been abrupt because I had, in the terms of my profession and experience, nothing to say. The star thrower was mad, and his particular acts were a folly with which I had not chosen to associate myself. I was an observer and a scientist. Nevertheless, I had seen the rainbow attempting to attach itself to earth.

On a point of land, as though projecting into a domain beyond us, I found the star thrower. In the sweet rain-swept morning, that great many-hued rainbow still lurked and wavered tentatively beyond him. Silently I sought and picked up a still-living star, spinning it far out into the waves. I spoke once briefly. "I understand," I said. "Call me another thrower." Only then I allowed myself to think, He is not alone any longer. After us there will be others.

We were part of the rainbow—an unexplained projection into the natural. As I went down the beach I could feel the drawing of a circle in men's minds, like that lowering, shifting realm of color in which the thrower labored. It was a visible model of something toward which man's mind had striven, the circle of perfection.

I picked and flung another star. Perhaps far outward on the rim of space a genuine star was similarly seized and flung. I could feel the movement in my body. It was like a sowing—the sowing of life on an infinitely gigantic scale. I looked back across my shoulder. Small and dark against the receding rainbow, the star thrower stooped and flung once more. I never looked again. The task we had assumed was too immense for gazing. I flung and flung again while all about us roared the insatiable waters of death.

But we, pale and alone and small in that immensity, hurled back
the living stars. Somewhere far off, across bottomless abysses, I felt
as though another world was flung more joyfully. I could have
thrown in a frenzy of joy, but I set my shoulders and cast, as the
thrower in the rainbow cast, slowly, deliberately, and well. The task
was not to be assumed lightly, for it was men as well as starfish
that we sought to save. For a moment, we cast on an infinite beach
together beside an unknown hurler of suns. It was, unsought, the
destiny of my kind since the rituals of the ice age hunters, when life
in the Northern Hemisphere had come close to vanishing. We had
lost our way, I thought, but we had kept, some of us, the memory of
the perfect circle of compassion from life to death and back again to
life—the completion of the rainbow of existence. Even the hunters
in the snow, making obeisance to the souls of the hunted, had
known the cycle. The legend had come down and lingered that he
who gained the gratitude of animals gained help in need from the
dark wood.

I cast again with an increasingly remembered sowing motion
and went my lone way up the beaches. Somewhere, I felt, in a great
atavistic surge of feeling, somewhere the Thrower knew. Perhaps he
smiled and cast once more into the boundless pit of darkness. Perhaps he, too, was lonely, and the end toward which he labored remained hidden—even as with ourselves.

I picked up a star whose tube feet ventured timidly among my
fingers while, like a true star, it cried soundlessly for life. I saw it
with an unaccustomed clarity and cast far out. With it, I flung myself as forfeit, for the first time, into some unknown dimension of
existence. From Darwin's tangled bank of unceasing struggle, self-
ishness, and death, had arisen, incomprehensibly, the thrower who
loved not man, but life. It was the subtle cleft in nature before
which biological thinking had faltered. We had reached the last
shore of an invisible island—yet, strangely, also a shore that the
primitives had always known. They had sensed intuitively that man
cannot exist spiritually without life, his brother, even if he slays.
Somewhere, my thought persisted, there is a hurler of stars, and he
walks, because he chooses, always in desolation, but not in defeat.

In the night the gas flames under the shelling kettles would continue to glow. I set my clock accordingly. Tomorrow I would walk
in the storm. I would walk against the shell collectors and the
flames. I would walk remembering Bacon's forgotten words "for

the uses of life." I would walk with the knowledge of the disconti-
nuities of the unexpected universe. I would walk knowing of the
rift revealed by the thrower, a hint that there looms, inexplicably,
in nature something above the role men give her. I knew it from
the man at the foot of the rainbow, the starfish thrower on the
beaches of Costabel.

Angle 1: Initial Response

Log Entry 1

Read through your double-entry log and review your initial impressions. How would you sum up your responses? For Log Entry 1,
make a summary statement about your first impressions of this
essay.

Angle 2: Story Threads

One of the ways we've already suggested that readers construct
meaning from demanding texts is to try to find connections between what is in the text and their own lives. Eiseley begins "The
Star Thrower" in a meditative way by suggesting that "there are
times when I have thought to read lessons in the sky, or in books,
or from the behavior of my fellows . . ."

Collaborating

Share with your group a time in your life when you learned something important. The experience may have occurred in school or
somewhere else; it may have happened in a strange, unexpected
way, as Eiseley's great lesson came to him from his experience on
the beach at Costabel.

Log Entry 2

Record in pictures and/or words any connections you have been able to make between lessons you have learned and the one Eiseley learned in "The Star Thrower."

Angle 3: Shifting Perspectives

Log Entry 3

Imagine that the star thrower was telling the story of his encounters with Eiseley on the beach at Costabel. What kind of person is the star thrower? Try to get inside his mind and write an interior monologue as he speculates about this encounter.

Collaborating

Share your monologue with other members of your group. Talk about the likenesses and differences in how each of you perceived this encounter.

Angle 4: Connecting with the Writer

As suggested earlier, it is often important to know something about the background of an essayist. In reading "The Star Thrower," you learn a great deal about Eiseley as a human being; it might be helpful to know a little more about his life, however. Eiseley was an anthropologist, but his interests ranged from evolution to the study of early peoples in America. He studied the flora and fauna as tools for dating evolutionary changes; he investigated the nature of animals and of human beings. Eiseley believed strongly in the need for what he called the "contemplative naturalist," a person who had time to observe, speculate, and dream. In another essay, "The Enchanted Glass," he wrote, "When the human mind exists in the light of reason and no more than reason, we may say with absolute certainty that a man and all that made him will be in that instant gone."

As you might expect of such a scientist, Eiseley's contemplations found their way into stories and poems as well as essays. His poem, "The Face of the Lion," may give you an additional perspective on his essay.

The Face of the Lion

Loren Eiseley

The moth-eaten lion with shoe-button eyes
is lumpy by modern standards
      and his mane
scarcely restorable.
   I held him in my arms
      when I was small.
I held him when my parents quarreled
as they did often while
     I shrank away.
     My beast has come
down the long traverse of such years and travel
      as have left outworn or lost
beds slept in, women loved, hall clocks that struck
     wrong hours,
     photographs
in years forgotten, notes, lovers' quarrels, dear God
      where go
our living hours,
    upon what windy ash heaps are they kept?
Down what sepulchral chambers must we creep
who seek the past?
    I who have dug through bones
and broken skulls and shards
     into the farther deeps
      rescind
such efforts now.
     I cannot practice
   the terrible archaeology of the brain
     nor plumb

one simple childhood thought. I want no light to shine
   into those depths forever
        but the lion
sits on the shelf above my desk
        and I,
          near-sighted now,
take comfort that he looks
       forthright and bold
         as when
my hands were small,
       as when
my brain received him living,
        something kind
         where little kindness was.

The mirror tells me that my hair is grey
but the wild animist within my heart
refuses to acknowledge him a toy
given by someone long ago
        forgotten.
No, no, the lion lives
      and watches me
as I do him.
        Should I forget
the hours in the blizzard dark,
       the tears
spilled silent while I clutched his mane?
He is very quiet there upon the shelf,
as I am here, but we were silent
       even then,
past words,
   past time.
      We waited for the light
and fell asleep when no light ever came.

      I do not
delude myself.
    The lion's face is slowly changing
    into the face of death
      but when I lie down
       upon my pillow
        in the final hour

I shall lie quietly and clutch
        the remnants of his mane.
            It happens we have known
a greater dark together
        he and I.
I am not terrified
        if he has come
            wearing another guise.
To him the watcher I will trust my sleep,
          shoe-button eyes, the lion on the shelf.

Collaborating

Discuss the poem with your group and talk about how the poem sheds light on the essay—if indeed you find that it does.

Log Entry 4

Record your ideas and those of your group. Use whatever form you find appropriate—notes, clusters, sketches.

Angle 5: Language and Craft

Graphic

One angle of vision that we've suggested can help a reader get an overall picture of a complex work—essay, poem, or story—is a map. To understand the language and craft of this essay, construct a map that shows how the essay develops. You may work alone or with a partner, and use any organizational pattern you find workable.

Begin by figuring out what you see as the central image or primary idea. (There is no "right" answer; you decide and then substantiate your decision with appropriate quotations on "spider webs" or mapping strands.) Feel free to use images, symbols, sketches, and drawings as they illustrate your concept of the whole essay—the language, the organization, and the ideas. As a suggestion, you might talk about the skull and the eye that appear in the epigraph and then recur throughout the essay. Or talk about starfish or walking on the beach when you feel overwhelmed by life.

Angle 6: Recasting the Text

Log Entry 5

Eiseley, as you know, wrote both poetry and prose. There are a lot of poems hidden in the essay. Select an image or an idea that you find provocative and read through the essay, recording words and phrases that pertain to the subject you have chosen. Then recast the essay into a poem or a sequence of poems. Don't try to include everything. Just focus on one image or idea for each poem you try, but limit yourself to Eiseley's words. Construct a meaningful poem. Give the poem a title, but again choose words for the title that you find somewhere in the essay.

Share your poems, and work together to refine them.

Angle 7: You, the Text, the World

It is important to know that you do not need to come to a conclusion about the meaning of a work of literature. You may need to form your ideas about the meaning a work has for you at a particular moment; another day, however, when you are in a different mood or have had an experience that relates to the events in a story, you may find that your understanding or envisionment of the story has changed.

Every step you take toward creating richer meaning involves changing perspectives, making connections, and facing new possibilities. You make interpretive decisions each time you look through a different lens. By looking at a work from different angles, your reading becomes more imaginative, intellectual, and emotional.

Collaborating

Read through your logs and think about the various activities you've done with this essay. Talk with your partner about how your understanding and appreciation of the essay have changed or deepened as you looked at it from different angles, as you have talked, written about, and mapped or drawn your ideas.

- What new questions can you ask now?

- Which angles of vision gave you the most insight and the most pleasure as you worked with this essay?

- What else can you say about the meaning of this essay?

Log Entry 6

Using your logs, the text, your own responses, and events in your own experience that you feel are relevant, reflect on the meaning this essay has for you now. Write your reflections as a short essay. You may accompany your essay with a graphic that conveys your ideas symbolically.

Building Your Course Portfolio

Review your log entries from this chapter to decide which ones might become portfolio entries. After you have selected, revised, and polished them, include them in your course portfolio. Refer to Chapter 1 for full instructions on preparing the portfolio and for written, graphic, and performance options that you could develop.

Complete your course portfolio by writing a preface in which you introduce yourself and your work. Also include a final self-assessment in which you detail how well you have met your initial goals and what additional goals you would like to achieve. Put this all together in a sturdy, attractive presentation package that celebrates your growth in inquiring, comprehending, and composing.

Index of Authors and Titles